THE RHETORIC OF FILM

THE RHETORIC OF FILM

JOHN HARRINGTON   *University of Massachusetts*

HOLT, RINEHART AND WINSTON, INC.

New York   Chicago   San Francisco   Atlanta
Dallas   Montreal   Toronto   London   Sydney

Copyright © 1973 by Holt, Rinehart and Winston, Inc.
All Rights Reserved
Library of Congress Catalog Card Number: 72–88131
ISBN: 0–03–088124–2
Printed in the United States of America
3 4 5 6   090   9 8 7 6 5 4 3 2 1

PREFACE

By the time a person is fourteen, he will witness 18,000 murders on the screen. He will also see 350,000 commercials. By the time he is eighteen, he will stockpile nearly 17,000 hours of viewing experience and will watch at least 20 movies for every book he reads. Eventually the viewing experience will absorb ten years of his life.

The better a person understands what happens during the process of viewing, the more perspective he is likely to have on a video murder, a plea to use Listerine, or an attempt to tamper with his political ideals. This text approaches film as an act of communication, providing the reader with the basic tools needed for alert participation in the viewing experience, while at the same time suggesting some of the bonds between cinema and other forms of communication and art. Most of us are well acquainted with what it means to sit passively in front of the screen and let images tumble over us. But there are many times when parts of the mind nag at us for being passive, and some impulse prods us to think and to respond. By understanding the tools and methods filmmakers use to create responses in audiences, we will be better prepared to interpret and deal actively with what we see.

It is easy to take for granted the ability to grapple with the rhetoric of film, much as many people take for granted the ability to play baseball, cook, swim, or backpack. But it must be noted that most people do not rely for long on their natural abilities in such activities but instead learn from other people (coaches, teachers, friends) or from books. Visual literacy, on the other hand, they often neglect. Although people watch movies constantly, few seek formal or informal help in dealing with visual communication. Ask any viewer if he understands *Citizen Kane* or *A Clockwork Orange* and he will most likely answer "yes" and give the matter no further thought.

To say that someone *understands* a movie, though, often means very little because his understanding might involve only an awareness of the plot line, while he might lose the meaning or import of a story completely. To understand the plot of *A Clockwork Orange,* for example, requires little beyond following the acts of a young man who loves violence; but what is the director, Stanley Kubrick, trying to say about his "hero's" violence and about society's response? The process of understanding works on several levels, and the more a person notices various levels in a film, the more he understands.

Even television's formula situation-comedies, westerns, or soap operas are not as easily understood as one might at first be tempted to think. The themes are usually more than obvious, but what about the emotions (concern, dislike, sorrow, and so on) the viewer feels—emotions that seem an easy task for a filmmaker to evoke? Why do *As the World Turns* and *Gunsmoke* have so many devotees? How about James Bond and Godzilla? And what about the ideological underpinnings of every movie—how do they work upon a viewer, affecting or molding his beliefs and attitudes? For example, how much of the attitude of Americans toward "foreigners" (Chinese, Russians, Laplanders, South Sea Islanders, Arabs) or of the middle aged toward leather-jacketed motorcyclists has been implanted or altered by portrayals in movies? From such a perspective, the need for understanding the nuances within film soon appears to be a matter relevant to the life of most individuals.

"Easily" understanding film rhetoric begins to look like a complex matter. And it should. If we are able to raise serious questions about low-grade movies—and even see them as defining a culture—we can expect highly sophisticated filmmakers to challenge us at every step. The more perceptive a viewer becomes about the various facets of film, the more he can hope to understand—rather than passively watch—what appears before him on the screen.

This text approaches the task of understanding the rhetoric of film from a viewer's perspective, as far as that is possible. Rather than telling someone how to make a film, the discussion focuses on those matters important to a viewer's ability to respond to and deal with what he meets during the viewing experience. A person does not need to learn the more technical aspects of filmmaking to perceive how films communicate, but it is essential that he know something about the filmmaker's basic rhetorical tools and strategies.

Because no common knowledge of a particular film or group of films can be assumed, references in this book to specific films have been kept to a minimum. Instead, most examples are hypothetical and self-contained so that a reader can understand how something works without necessarily having recently seen a particular film. Once various techniques and methods are understood, the reader can quickly spot them at work in whatever films he happens to see. References to specific films have also been used sparingly because the person just beginning to study film is justifiably intimidated by a barrage of allusions, names, and titles that have little or no meaning to him and hence tend to limit his understanding rather than to enhance it.

An understanding of the principles of film rhetoric provides a viewer with two important skills. First, he can more easily notice and respond to blatant forms of media manipulation. Whether he encounters a politician seeking a vote or a detergent company trying to gain a customer, the viewer will be better able to spot a persuader's ploys. Second, the viewer who knows something about the rhetoric of film will also be able to watch films with more appreciation, understanding, and awareness of implications. He can begin enjoying greater insight into those films that seem difficult because a film artist is trying something new or attempting to say something complicated. Hence an understanding of the rhetoric of film adds both to a viewer's perception of the persuasive aspects of the medium and to his enjoyment of film art.

J.H.

Amherst, Massachusetts
November 1972

ACKNOWLEDGMENTS

I owe many thanks for help in writing this book. Some of those to whom I am indebted are Jane Ross of Holt, Rinehart and Winston; Phil Leininger; James Shokoff of the State University of New York at Fredonia; the University of Massachusetts for a summer grant; Eugene Walz and Charles Eidsvik of the University of Massachusetts; Connie and Larry Miller; and, most of all, Marie, Brendan, and Maura Harrington.

Photographs by J. Paul Kirouac

CONTENTS

THE RHETORIC OF FILM

RHETORIC AND FILM

Language is the means of expressing or communicating thoughts or feelings. It works not only to convey lofty thoughts, but also at the level of the inarticulate sounds of animals expressing basic needs. A simple grunt, human or animal, or a thumb held in the air is language if the **sender** tries to say something to a **receiver.** Even a flip of the wrist is a kind of language in some instances, and one could speak of the "language of wrist flipping," limited though that language might be. A person need not look far to see a world full of languages, from the language of road signs to that of music or of mathematics. Although the term "language" first calls to mind such spoken and written languages as English, French, or Hindi, these represent only complex versions of but one language category—**verbal** language.

Any identifiable form of communication molds its unique language or combinations of languages, bringing to life terms and structures vital to its users. Communication among people is consequently a much more complicated matter than arranging words into proper grammatical sentences. Every act of communication involves one or more languages operating simultaneously, and the sender of a message must take care to coordinate all of them. In normal conversation, for example, the sender

1

must control not only the actual words of spoken English, but also such matters as enunciation and "body language" (which includes physical bearing and mannerisms as well as gestures). Depending on the circumstances, an affected lisp can establish a point effectively or make a speaker sound like a fool, while a jabbing finger can drive home a point or evoke audience hostility by seeming too condescending. Even on paper, words are not the sole aspect of communication—style of type or handwriting, kind of paper, neatness, or even diagrams are language components altering and transforming a sender's message.

So complicated are the inputs from various types of languages that mastery of any one offers no guarantee of even adequate performance in apparently related aspects of communication. Experience reveals this to most of us in the difference between our spoken and written communication. Often those who have mastered many of the nuances of spoken English become paralyzed when facing a writing assignment. And many who write fluently are stage-struck when they must use spoken language to communicate. Nevertheless, languages work in similar ways even though occurring in a great variety of forms. The broad principles of communication, especially those of rhetoric, apply equally well to spoken English, to body language, or to the languages of film.

RHETORIC

Rhetoric is a "how to" area of study focusing on ways of putting together the various components and complexities of languages in order to bring about effective communication. Hence rhetoric deals mainly with the way a sender's message will influence a receiver.

Occasionally "rhetoric" is a nasty word. Such phrases as "mere rhetoric" and "it's only rhetoric" belittle whatever they are applied to. In everyday usage "rhetoric" often implies deception and falsehood rather than honesty and truth and suggests that something has style without substance, like the tinseled facades of Hollywood movie sets. As William Butler Yeats once complained, "sentimentality is deceiving one's self; rhetoric is deceiving other people."

But rhetoric is not inherently deceiving. Human communication could not work if founded on deceit, yet every statement originates from a particular rhetorical stance. Only our own paranoia would lead us to see a world offering nothing but conspiracies of everyday communication based on ulterior purposes. Although a good deal of intentional deception obviously occurs in our society, we can safely assume that most people manipulate languages in order to communicate rather than to deceive. Since people must use rhetorical tools to reach each other, we should not take too narrow a view of a study of the methods of effective communication. The misuses of rhetoric are only too blatant, but sloppy thinking and articulation probably cause more falsehood in communication than does outright chicanery.

Rhetoric is not a study of ethics but of the art of communicating. Ethical judgments must be applied to the uses of rhetoric, but it does not inherently work for either good or evil ends, just as science does not. Both must undergo ethical scrutiny, as must every other matter affecting people, but the tool must not be confused with the final product. Rhetoric, like science, should be treated skeptically, and we must constantly apply ethical judgments to the many forms of rhetoric confronting us in daily life. But the focus of such efforts is not on the evils of rhetoric per se but rather on the relationship and interdependence of tool or method and final product. The first step to sound ethical judgment is to achieve an understanding of what rhetoric is and how it influences people.

Rhetoric began as a practical and necessary art, and its purpose has remained constant—to convince. Consequently, rhetoric deals with the effectiveness of communication and manifests itself in every mode of language. We can speak of a rhetoric of fiction, of journalism, of documentary, of public speaking, and so on. **Persuasion** is traditionally the key word associated with rhetoric. One person attempts to persuade someone else to believe or do something. But such a statement helps only slightly to define rhetoric because communication almost automatically involves persuasion. A person would be hard pressed to offer an example of a statement that does not lead someone to an attitude toward something. Even a statement such as "the water is hot" works to convince. It does little good to use the word "persuasion" as if it referred to a huge propaganda machine cranking out lies to feed flaccid brains. Almost by definition, communication goes hand in hand with persuasion. It is the motive for—not the presence of—persuasion that legitimately causes people alarm.

Through rhetoric a sender attempts to control a receiver's responses. If a person smiles and talks pleasantly to a policeman who has stopped him for speeding, that person expects a different response from the officer than open hostility would draw. Yet people seldom consciously think out their responses ahead of time. Instead, a good many of one's impulses to send rhetorical signals to others, as well as the signals themselves, have been instilled during childhood, and a person initiates and responds to rhetorical nuances with little conscious thought. Usually a "thank you" is simply a conditioned response to an act of kindness and contains no real content as a statement, yet its inclusion affects the person for whom it is meant. And its absence also communicates something very strongly.

In other cases, senders carefully calculate and control their rhetorical presentations. Advertisements present the most obvious examples, and advertisers are among the most frequent practitioners of deceptive rhetoric in our society. Because advertisers use rhetorical devices in a conscious and manipulative way, we usually call their work "propaganda." They use every possible emotional ploy to make us buy their product or look favorably upon their company. Even the federal government recognizes the deceptive rhetoric of advertising and has begun making advertisers prove their claims.

Politicians, of course, must also receive credit for being among the heaviest abusers of rhetoric. Both those in politics and those who comment on political matters usually seem more concerned with promoting a particular viewpoint than with sorting out "truth." By playing upon emotions and prejudices (radical, liberal, or conservative), politicos (in all senses) hope to win hearts and minds. Similarly, much of the conventional fare produced for theater or television relies on well-established formulas for pulling our heartstrings, making us "like" or "buy" their product. Who fails to respond to a brave marshal facing down five tough hombres? Or to a little girl lost in the welter of a big city? Or to a "love story" in which the illness and death of a sweet young bride destroy a beautiful and heartwarming marriage?

But there is also a rhetorical situation that falls between conditioned responses and deliberate manipulation of feeling and emotion. In many instances artists, as well as other people, think of themselves as communicators simply trying to express their thoughts or feelings. They have no conscious thoughts of "persuading" anyone in the devious sense of the word, yet they do try to convey something. A film such as *Dream of the Wild Horses,* for example, develops a slow-motion cine-poem showing horses running through water; the result is a film of beautiful, graceful movement, but no real "point" exists.

Similarly, I do not think I have any particular ax to grind in writing this book, nor do I intend to trick anyone into believing anything. Rather, I have something to say that I hope will bring some understanding about the methods of the film medium. Yet I am influencing just by writing and conveying a message. And I do wish to make a number of points. I want to persuade the reader to look at rhetoric and film in certain ways, convinced that my ways are the best ways. They may not be, but I am writing and persuading in the belief that they are.

The midground of rhetoric—between unconscious response and blatant manipulation—is the most fertile area for those concerned with communication. This is the ground where most honest attempts to say or show something grow, and where most people try to understand and apply what they see and hear. It is also this ground where the artist plants his seeds. Whether in print or on film, the artist in a chaotic world uses rhetorical techniques to make sense of experience for himself and for others.

SPEAKER, AUDIENCE, AND SUBJECT

Aristotle clarified the basic lines of rhetoric by distinguishing among the three components of a communication: the speaker (voice or sender), the audience (receiver), and the subject. Diagramed, the relationship looks like this:

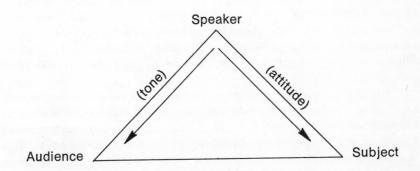

The speaker defines his relationship to his audience through **tone** (respectful, affectionate, chastising, cajoling) and to his subject through **attitude** (firm, investigative, favorable, unfavorable, knowledgeable, uncertain). He must be careful to treat his subject at the level of his audience and be sure that his audience is the proper one for his subject. Such a speaker, or voice, can obviously present only one face to his audience, and hence he must always be distinguished from the *person* undertaking a communication. The speaker represents only one face of a multifaceted personality—a face adapted to the needs of a particular situation. As Aristotle suggests, the person who wishes to communicate must adopt a voice with a style and manner presenting a subject in a way most pleasing to an audience.

Because a reader cannot know for certain the motives of a writer, a listener those of a speaker, or an audience those of a filmmaker, we can do little to distinguish intentional from unintentional persuasion or propaganda. All we can ever really cling to is the film or book or ad or painting or cartoon at hand. Motives are invisible. We cannot fully know what goes on in another person's mind. Rather, we must be sensitive to the manner of communication: critical and questioning in response to those directly trying to convince us; thoughtful about the daily pressures from media; and perceptive of the techniques and methods of art and communication that are part of our lives. Rhetorical language implicitly or explicitly urges people to action, and we must carefully consider the how and why of that action.

THE INTERPLAY OF LANGUAGES

Rhetoric involves the complex use of one or more languages. Some commentators like to speak of "the language of film" as a real and definable entity with components resembling those of major verbal languages such as English or French. Such an analogy works best if we conceive of film as having a single, unified language. At the same time, isolating a single language of film is an impossible task. Although several languages operate simultaneously in daily conversations or in printed literature, the components of the major language—spoken or written—can be hunted down and artificially distinguished. We usually do this for English by applying rules of Latin grammar (and the result is often absurd).

But in film a single dominant language cannot be separated from the multiplicity of contributing languages. The number of potentially strong language contributors to film, each with its own grammar and syntax, makes it necessary to think in terms of the *languages* used in film rather than in terms of the single or dominant language. Many of these languages are readily evident: the language of subtitles, of dialogue, of narration, of visual images, of symbols, of lighting, of music, and so on. The dynamics of film depend not upon the effective use of a single language, but upon the complex interplay of many languages often making apparently contradictory statements. These languages unite to form the rhetoric of film.

Writers on the "language of film" fondly speak of film's grammar and syntax. Since such discussions build on our existing knowledge of languages, they are indeed helpful—as long as we regard them as analogies used to grasp the workings of film communication. Most languages depend on stringing together various elements until a thought or feeling finds expression. Grammar studies the way units of communication work to create a structure (such as a sentence or a paragraph). Syntax is a subheading of grammar dealing specifically with the way segments (words, in verbal language) unite and are ordered to form larger units.

Film is a complex form of communication relying on putting things together simultaneously and sequentially. The impact of film depends on a medley of sounds (background noises, music, dialogue) and visuals (many small segments of film spliced together) combined so that each will have meaning in terms of and because of other sounds and visuals. Consequently, many factors contribute to the rhetoric of a film, forming an organized unit of sounds and images communicating to an audience the ideas and feelings of the filmmaker. Each language making up a film has a grammar and syntax of its own, yet all the parts functioning in a film contribute to what could be called, by analogy to other forms of communication, "the grammar and syntax of film." It is, however, the complex interplay of all elements of aural and visual languages that establishes a film's rhetorical form.

REPRESENTING REALITY

Like the rhetoric of spoken languages or the rhetoric of written languages, the rhetoric of film has basic comprehensible principles and an orderly way of approaching a subject. All languages must rely on abstraction as tools of communication. As Ernst Cassirer suggests, man is a symbol-using animal distinguished by the power of intelligence and by the ability to use symbols to communicate his thoughts. Spoken language was one of the earliest developments in the search for self-expression. Words were used to represent things or actions: A sound stood for a thing (such as a tree) or an action (such as running). The alphabet added yet another method for representing things or actions.

Film extends man's ability to use abstractions and symbols as tools of communication. Film simultaneously works—and works effectively—on both concrete and abstract levels. Obviously film is an extraordinarily specific and sensory medium: We hear "real" sounds and we see "real" people and objects. Unlike passages of prose description evoking images and sounds, film displays sights and sounds that seem real.

The word "seem," however, is important for we must remember that what we see *represents* reality and hence is also abstraction. What we see on the screen is not reality. A distinction between the sensory reality of images and sounds and the reality of the world may seem obvious enough while one is sitting in a corner reading a book or climbing a mountain, but the distinction appears less obvious when a person is engrossed in the film experience.

Film, like print literature, requires that we willingly "suspend disbelief"—to use Coleridge's phrase for the process of making ourselves respond to literary language—as if it were "reality." Yet film needs no Coleridge to urge viewers to suspend disbelief. Instead, film involves the viewer in such a sensory manner that he seems to gain most by being asked at times to refuse to suspend disbelief. Perhaps this is what modern filmmakers (such as Ingmar Bergman in *The Passion of Anna*) try to tell us when they include a shot in which an actor interrupts a scene to explain his feelings toward the character he is playing, a camera jiggles noticeably at an inappropriate place, or the mechanics of photography otherwise remind a viewer that he is observing art, not reality.

The figures who seem so real when viewed on a screen are never real people acting out their lives in full dimensionality—not even in documentary. The viewer always watches a preselected representative sample of some aspect of life; actors represent certain things, using gestures, expressions, and environmental relations to reveal feelings and ideas about a character or subject. Although actors appear before the viewer as concrète visible and auditory images, they represent feelings and ideas at the same time, hence existing both as concrete images and as abstractions. A character acting out "brotherly love" portrays an abstraction of brotherly love just as the word-pair is itself an abstraction.

The visual images and sounds of cinema have an intensity rarely found in daily life. A viewer often feels he knows a chief character better in ninety minutes than he knows his best friends after years. A filmmaker so carefully selects details to reveal character traits that a viewer forgets that the details are representative and that a person's psyche cannot possibly be explored in an hour and a half. As he watches *The Graduate,* for example, a viewer feels he knows Benjamin well, but the viewer actually knows Ben only as a representative of certain adolescent problems. While appearing to be a real person with an autonomous existence, Ben is also an abstraction making statements through the illustrations of an actor's movements. And so is almost every character in almost every film.

Part of cinema's great success comes from its ability to look deceptively simple. We almost always think we know where we are in a film—and how we got there. We trust our eyes, for we suppose that we witness the events on which ideas and conclusions are built. But the simplicity of film is indeed deceptive. The languages making up a film—and hence governing our emotional and intellectual responses—form an extraordinarily complex rhetorical unit.

FILM'S BASIC VISUAL UNITS: THE FRAME

Since film is primarily a visual medium, the grammar and syntax governing the stream of cinema's visual imagery are of first importance. The visual grammar and syntax of film concern the ways a filmmaker arranges shots into scenes and scenes into sequences, just as the grammar and syntax of spoken and written languages deal with the way words are arranged into sentences and sentences into paragraphs.

The smallest discernible unit in film is the **frame**. A frame is a single photographic image printed on a length of film.[1] A viewer can see

[1] In normal usage a *frame* differs from a *still*. A still is a photograph taken with a still (versus motion) camera and printed on photographic paper. Most pictures displayed outside theaters or appearing in newspaper ads or magazine articles are taken with still cameras on a movie's set and are made to be photographs standing alone even though an almost identical frame might appear in a film. Note the difference in a person's response to a still before and after viewing a film. Afterwards he has a context, and the still reminds him of a piece of action—it is part of a continuous stream of images. Before a person sees a film, he views the same photograph as an independent composition, considered in terms of itself. The stream of images of a film conditions a viewer's later responses.

a single frame only under certain artificial conditions: when a projector is stopped at "still" position; when a frame is excerpted and projected as a slide or printed on photographic paper; or when a freeze-frame appears on the screen.[2] Like a single letter in a word, a frame is not a part of a viewer's perceptions until it is isolated. Even then, it seldom has meaning.

Although a single photographic frame cannot be discerned during actual viewing, it contributes to a larger unit and is understood in terms of that unit. During normal projection, twenty-four frames per second (approximately a foot and a half of 35-mm film) pass through the projector's gate. Each image flashes on the screen, then the screen turns black and is followed by another frame. However, the human eye misses the period of blackout since the eye retains an image one-tenth of a second longer than the image exists. It is this physiological phenomenon that allows motion pictures to be seen in continuous movement with no apparent jumps or single frames visible. (Take two frames out of a shot, however, and the eye can often detect a jump.) The average feature contains close to 130,000 separate frames.

The word "frame" also has another meaning in the filmmaker's jargon. The frame is the outer boundary of a projected image—the lines of the rectangle on the screen where an image ends and blackness begins. Because the frame serves as the boundary of an image, it is the starting point in the filmmaker's composition. The camera itself sees indiscriminately. The filmmaker must make a variety of choices to be sure that he will put boundaries around a segment of experience that, when projected, will have meaning for the viewer.

THE SHOT

At a normal projection speed of twenty-four frames per second, it is quickly evident that a large number of frames make up the basic perceivable unit of the film, the **shot**. A shot is a single uninterrupted action of a camera.[3] Like the verbal word, the cinematic shot is the smallest functional unit of filmmaking. Some shots last only one or two frames,

---

[2] A *freeze-frame* is produced mechanically in a laboratory by printing the same frame over and over until the image on the screen resembles a projected slide. Actually, the viewer does not see a single frame during a freeze-frame; rather, he sees a repetition of the same picture, although his eye cannot detect any difference between a projected frame and a freeze-frame.

[3] A *take* is also a single uninterrupted action of a camera, but a take is the unedited footage and is seen from the point of view of the filmmaker rather than of the viewer. A take will frequently be shortened at both ends, and perhaps another shot or two will be cut into the middle creating three, four, five, or more shots out of a single take. For instance, during an interview two cameras might be trained on the two persons talking. Later, an editor will cut and splice to alternate between the two speakers, creating many separate shots from only two takes.

although such short shots appear rarely in commercial films. But anyone who has seen experimental films (such as Charles Braverman's *An American Time Capsule* or *The World of '68*) knows how rapidly shots can operate and how many shots the eye will accept in a small amount of time. Although longer shots are "standard," few last over thirty seconds. The exceptions, of course, run for as long as a filmmaker chooses to keep film running through his camera. The average shot runs from about two to thirty seconds.

Because it is the smallest functional unit of film and combines to form a larger statement, the shot syntactically parallels the word of spoken and written communication. The frame, on the other hand, resembles the single phoneme or letter of a word. Shots make up the vocabulary that film's visual grammar and syntax connect into statements with meaning. The vocabulary of film is primarily the vocabulary of a series of photographic images.

It is illuminating to consider the notion "shot" in relation to the notion "word" in order to grasp the syntactical workings of the basic unit of cinematic composition. The shots of a film draw meaning from their context much as words derive significance almost exclusively from their linguistic context. When isolated, the meaning of either a word or a shot is imprecise at best. Consider the word "stand." Is it a verb (such as a command to assume a certain physical position, or a description of what someone is doing or did do) or is it a noun (such as an ideological position one takes, a structure to sit on, a courtroom place of witness, or a group of trees)? Without a context, one cannot ascertain meaning or function. Similarly, a single shot has meaning, but without a context a particular meaning is difficult to identify. Consider, for example, a frame showing a saloon with men drinking at tables while a man stands just outside the swinging doors. Is the situation comical or threatening? Or are we seeing a typical Tuesday afternoon at Hank's saloon?

While analogies can be drawn between shot and word, the shot also resembles the written paragraph. A paragraph normally articulates an idea, then offers supportive evidence or arguments. Similarly, a shot in context assumes a general idea or mood and also offers many equivalents of simple declarative and descriptive sentences, providing a viewer with supportive information. Imagine the elements of a hypothetical shot put into statement form: The woman sits in the kitchen. The baby is in the highchair. The baby is crying. The woman is holding baby food. The wall is yellow. On the wall stands a picture of a horse. There is a table in the foreground. The table is round. The table is dark. There are four chairs around the table. All this, and far more, a viewer perceives as he watches a shot. A shot, like a paragraph, offers both detailed information and an idea or mood.

Any direct analogy between the shot and the paragraph, however, will quickly break down. The elements of a paragraph are met with one at a time. They are linear. The content of a shot is, for all practical purposes, available all at once.[4] Ideas and details are not easily separated. Abstract ideas are seldom stated as such in film—and then usually in documentaries. Film argues almost entirely by evidence, inexorably forcing a viewer to supply appropriate abstract ideas. We are not told, for instance, that Mr. Jones loves his wife. We *see* him love her. Film is a visual medium, and it must make its statements visually.

Shots are categorized according to the apparent closeness of the camera to the person or object photographed. With the early single focal length lenses, distance literally became the factor determining the "length" of a shot. With the present variety of lenses, only the illusion of distance counts. If an object or person seems very far away, the result is normally called an **extreme long-shot** (ELS), also called an **establishing shot** because it places objects in context and prepares a viewer for a closer look later. If a person or object appears extremely close, the shot is called an **extreme close-up** (ECU). In between lie the **long-shot** (LS), **medium long-shot** (MLS), **medium shot** (MS), **medium close-up** (MCU), and **close-up** (CU).

The distinctions among shots by distance are relative, and no precise lines or measurements separate the various shots. Usually, the human figure provides the chief standard for measurement. In an **extreme long-shot** a person might be visible, but the setting clearly dominates. The same person fills a good part of the vertical line of the frame in a **long-shot,** although the setting also receives strong emphasis. A **medium long-shot** reveals about three-fourths of the subject, while a **medium shot** (also called a mid-shot) would show the subject only from the waist up, focusing a viewer's attention more on the subject than on the setting but maintaining a clear relationship between the two. A **medium close-up** shows a person from the shoulders up, and a **close-up** shows only the head. An **extreme close-up** reveals only a small part of the face, such as the nose or an eye. (Figures 1a–g.)

What is a close-up in one situation, however, can be a mid- or long-shot in another. The length of a shot depends on the subject of a film (or of an individual scene). The longer a shot is, the more it shows of the subject; the shorter a shot is, the more it emphasizes detail that is part of the subject. Hence, the length of a shot is relative and depends upon what the filmmaker has chosen for a subject. If, for example, a film is about cities of the world, a shot of a red double-decker bus in London would be a close-up. The same shot would be a long-shot in a film about London's buses, while a shot of an instrument panel would be a close-up.

---

[4] Some shots do, of course, reveal certain components of content linearly; for example, a moving camera presents different pieces of information in a defined order.

Fig. 1a. *Extreme long-shot.* Note how background becomes less important with increasingly close shots, while character and expression become more important.

Fig. 1b.   *Long-shot.*

Fig. 1c. *Medium long-shot.*

Fig. 1d. *Medium shot.*

Fig. 1e. *Medium close-up.*

Fig. 1f.   *Close-up.*

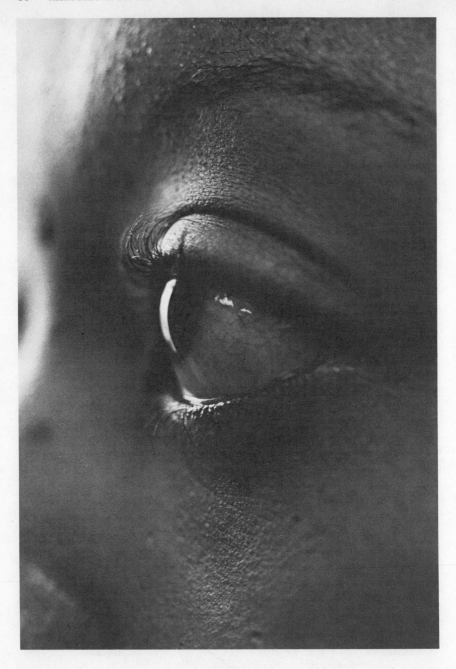

Fig. 1g.   *Extreme close-up.* Context is highly significant for close-ups and extreme close-ups because background does not help a viewer define what he sees.

THE SCENE

A filmmaker puts shots together to make up a scene. A **scene** is a series of shots that the viewer perceives as taken at the same location during a rather brief period of time. The classic western gunfight furnishes a good example of a scene. Some action prompts two men to face each other, one draws, the other follows suit, and one is killed or wounded. The gunfight might be preceded by a number of shots in the same location, and the scene typically ends quickly after the fight, with action resuming at another time or location.

Film scenes vary greatly in length. Sometimes a scene will be only a single shot long; in other cases a whole movie will have but one scene. Usually, however, scenes last for several minutes. Cinematic scenes tend to be much more crisp than scenes from plays (which offer the nearest literary analogue to cinematic scenes). The average film contains far more scenes than the average play. Since a filmmaker can cut instantly to another scene, he need not worry (as must a dramatist) about moving his cast on and off the stage and about scenery changes. A cinematic scene need last no longer than it takes the filmmaker to convey a single point.

THE SEQUENCE

The largest unit of film's visual grammar is the **sequence.** The nearest literary analogues to the sequence are the chapters of novels or the acts of plays. A number of scenes make up a sequence, which is the largest working unit of a film. A sequence is usually composed of a series of scenes that are related in location, time, generating action, point of view, or cast. At one time sequences were clearly set off by strong punctuation marks such as the fade-out and fade-in. These strong forms of punctuation alerted a viewer that a major segment of a film had ended and that a new one was about to begin. Contemporary filmmakers, however, have abandoned such obvious punctuation marks, relying instead on jump cuts[5] or other forms of transition.

A sequence provides an enlarged context to which individual shots and scenes contribute. Individual shots must always be read in terms of surrounding shots, and scenes must be considered in relation to other scenes. Our mental expectations when viewing film lead us to read all actions in terms of what precedes them. In the case of a gunfight, a film-

---

[5] A *jump cut* is an instantaneous shift from one action to another, at first seemingly unrelated, action. A cut from Paris in 1813 to New York in 1972, with no apparent transition, would normally constitute a jump cut. Such cuts rely upon the audience to fill in missing information and allow a filmmaker to move action rapidly forward through ellipses. Once a viewer consciously or unconsciously fills in missing information, the paradoxical unrelatedness of the two separate actions is, of course, resolved.

maker would normally include a number of significant scenes before the gunfight to enable us to read the actions properly. By the time of the gunfight we are set to respond in a certain way to its occurrence and its outcome. A sequence, then, provides a self-contained unit that can undergo evaluation and criticism.

Frame, shot, scene, and **sequence** are the most basic terms in the lexicon of film. They suggest the fundamental structures with which film operates, and they indicate the complex "cut-and-paste" nature of the medium. The rhetoric of any film grows from the way a filmmaker manipulates these basic structural units.

IDEA AND EXAMPLE:
RECORDING VISUAL REALITY

GENERALIZATION AND DETAIL

Take hunger. It is easier to visualize it in personal terms. "About a month and a half ago," Senator Mondale (D, Minn.) told the McGovern Committee, "I went to a small elementary area school in our small ghetto in St. Paul. They had a splendid cafeteria and a very balanced meal, a warm meal, salad, and about every fifth child could not afford it. One child, whom I will never forget as long as I live, was about six or seven years old. She had a filthy dress on, and she sat at this table amidst the other children eating their good meal, eating a chocolate cookie. She had a little dirty bag that she brought, that her mother had sent, and two other chocolate cookies. And I asked the principal, how can this happen? And he said, 'We still don't have the money to pay for lunches when the families can't afford it.' I assume there are millions like her in the country, that sit amidst their friends at lunch who have a decent meal, and they don't. It's a disgrace."

That hungry kid with three cookies at school represents America. The U.S. has six percent of the world's population and about half the world's resources but an income distribution, as noted in the Esterlys' *Freedom from Dependence* . . . that awards 77 percent of total income to the top half of the population and only 23 percent to the lower half.[1]

[1] "Tick, Tick, Tick," *The New Republic*, May 29, 1971, p. 6.

The two foregoing paragraphs are part of a short essay on America's social problems. Note the two different kinds of information conveyed in each paragraph. The first details what one person has seen and heard; the second provides statistics. Both make generalizations about hunger, but each proceeds in a unique way.

The second paragraph reveals print doing what it is best at—dealing with ideas not perceptible through the senses. "Six percent" cannot be seen, especially when the six percent represents the world's population. Nor can a statement about half the world's resources be grasped by the senses. Only through the imagination's ability to abstract can we comprehend the sweeping information of such a paragraph.

Juxtaposed with statistics involving the entire world, the situation of the little girl with a chocolate cookie should not mean much. But it does, and the writer of the article devotes far more words to the situation of one small person than to broad statements about the world. Yet the world, not the individual, concerns him most. Whatever the psychological reasons, visualization "in personal terms" creates greater impact than facts outside the pale of experience.

Consider what would occur if we were to translate the two paragraphs above into film. The type of information in paragraph two could be conveyed only through verbal languages. To present statistics on film would require either a narrator or the actual showing of words and figures on the screen. Only the "hungry kid with three cookies" could be a visual image on film, but the image would not say the same thing as the sentence.

Contrast the difficulties of filming the second paragraph with the ease of filming the first. Senator Mondale's words start from a distance and move in on the subject almost like the opening shots of a typical documentary: city, ghetto, elementary school, cafeteria, meal, four children eating, one child not eating much. Each movement discovers a progressively individual detail. The age of the child, her dress, the place she sits, her chocolate cookie, and her dirty bag—all provide images the camera can readily record. Even the principal could be recorded on film, as could Senator Mondale himself.

Visualizing detail is what film does best. By stringing together a series of details, such as those found in paragraph one, a filmmaker spawns an idea. Although occasionally letting ideas emerge from piled-up detail, print usually relies on stated generalizations. Of course, an abstract idea can be stated verbally on film (we can imagine Senator Mondale saying "It's a disgrace"), but verbal statement is often unnecessary if the filmmaker does his job properly. Ideas emerge from the details presented. If the visuals do their job, further statement is not only uninteresting, it can be self-defeating.

One of the most important ideas to grasp about film is that in it ideas need not—usually should not—be expressed verbally. Film is primarily a visual medium and must rely on images to convey ideas. Images, of course, are also fundamental in written language, but print images function somewhat differently from film images. On the first level of meaning in either print or film, an image attempts to reproduce literally a sensory experience or object. On a secondary level, images are associative and figurative. An image of a coffin is an image of a box with a unique shape; it is also an image connoting death. The linguistic context of the image will normally cause a number of additional associations. (For example, the coffin might raise associations because the audience knows that the coffin holds the hero's wife, who died in the burning house trying to save her three small children.)

Print and film handle images differently at each level, however. A writer can reproduce an image only in a selective and largely abstract way. He tries to create mental pictures, but even the best writers succeed only partially. Through photography, on the other hand, a filmmaker can reproduce an image in toto with all details visible, allowing a viewer to see with his own eyes. Yet the writer has great potential for associations and allusion, while the filmmaker must work hard to make viewers aware of associational meanings beyond what might be viewed in daily life.

Even though effective prose uses concrete examples and words that a reader can visualize in his imagination, print thrives on abstraction. Abstraction allows a writer to say things that are not verifiable through sensory means. Ironically, the less tied to the physical world, the more plausible most abstraction seems. The more difficult something is to see and touch, the more difficult it is to refute. If someone tells you that your arm is covered with mud, you can quickly verify the statement. If, on the other hand, someone tells you that most people dislike you, there is no speedy way to verify or disprove the charge, and it will linger in your mind. Film, however, depends on "statements" that can be seen and, to a certain degree, verified (although the rhetoric of film depends on viewers accepting images as "true").

Details selected from experience provide the most common source of evidence in communication. To communicate effectively in either print or film, one must find the bricks and mortar that will build his case. But film has an edge in using detail since film captures images realistically but can directly photograph neither an idea nor a generalization. By definition, a generalization is something that applies to a wide variety of things simultaneously (usually within a certain class). Film, however, can capture only the particular. In print one can say "all daffodils are yellow"; visually, film can only show a series of shots of yellow daffodils and let the viewer come to the conclusion that "all daffodils are yellow." Or a filmmaker might show many different shots of yellow daffodils juxtaposed with shots of various other flowers appearing in different colors. For example: yellow daffodil/red rose/yellow daffodil/yellow rose/yellow daffodil/pink rose/yellow daffodil/white rose, and so on. Film is a medium that manipulates images in order to generate ideas, hence making visual images into important bearers of generalizations as well as of details.

A sense of the way film creates ideas out of detailed images was the contribution of the great Russian filmmakers Vsevolod Pudovkin and Sergei Eisenstein. Although they differed about how and why, they both demonstrated that montage is primarily responsible for creating ideas in film. Although the word "montage" has other applications in film, it usually suggests a rhetorical method of juxtaposing and arranging shots to produce an idea—that is, something greater than the shots in isolation are able to say. For example, consider these three shots: a plate heaped with steaming, appetizing food; a little girl, about six or seven, wearing a filthy dress and staring at the camera with an expressionless face; and the same little girl with a smile. If a filmmaker first shows the expressionless girl followed by the food and then the smiling face, the viewer assumes that the hungry girl has been offered the food and is now happy. Reverse the order: smiling face, food, expressionless face. The filmmaker has now depicted disappointment and despair. If he puts the food first followed rapidly by the smiling girl then the expressionless face, the effect is one of hope followed by resignation. If he moves from food to the expressionless girl and then to the smiling girl, the result is realization (she suddenly realizes that the food is for her). Put the food last and rearrange the shots of the girl and still other meanings are possible. Of course, all of these meanings depend on context. Earlier shots in the film will condition the viewer's responses to the three shots. Filmmakers develop ideas by juxtaposing a few shots and then building and expanding with ensuing shots.

Since films seldom generalize through verbal language, the importance of the image as a carrier of thought must not be underestimated. Sounds and visual images provide raw details; their linkage creates complex ideas. The filmmaker's first concern is for the quality of his original image; editing, added sound, or special effects cannot salvage images that do not reveal the depth and breadth of what the filmmaker examines. It is the director's task to design and prepare the images recorded by the camera, and he must both photograph what is significant in a subject and control the viewer's eye movements at all times.

COMPOSITION IN STASIS

Composition is one of the key elements a director uses to control a viewer's perception of details. Although composition involves every factor contributing to the physical presence of a shot (perspective, lighting, and so on), we must focus for now on the arrangement of objects and movements a director uses to make a viewer see certain things.

Composition creates a sense of depth—both physical and psychological—to draw the viewer into what occurs within the frame. Largely through composition a viewer willingly suspends a knowledge that what he sees is two dimensional and willingly accepts the semblance of reality before him. Since film speaks only in the present tense, each shot is an action word—a verb propelling the action in a particular direction. Hence the key to composition is *motion,* either actual or implied.

Traditionally, discussions of composition apply only to images in stasis (without physical movement) such as paintings or photographs. To call a painting static is a criticism. An artist must provide a *sense* of motion, encouraging the human eye to move in patterns across a fixed landscape. Although film looks first for *real* motion, the director must still place people and objects in certain relationships within the frame to prepare for psychological lines of motion. (The "frame" in this sense is the physical side, top, and bottom limits that a viewer sees as the fixed rectangle of the projected image.)

The human eye is directed by lines and positioning as they are related to other lines and masses. Vertical lines seem to soar, and the human eye expectantly follows their uplifting energy. Horizontals imply stability and solidity. Diagonals usually convey feelings of confusion, division, or incompleteness. A director synchronizes the dominant lines of what he shoots with the mood he wishes to create.

The frame has definite and fixed limits, and a filmmaker can do little to change its shape. A still photographer, by contrast, can escape the fixed frame of his instrument and make a picture in almost any shape. If he wants to emphasize the soaring quality of a Gothic cathedral, he will make his picture much taller than it is wide by cropping (cutting) away unwanted material. For all practical purposes, a filmmaker cannot crop but must add as many secondary movements as possible to his horizontal rectangle. Of course, a wide screen helps establish the horizontal lines needed for panorama (the impression of an almost unlimited view in all directions along the horizon), thus giving a filmmaker some control over horizontal composition. But the wide screen has trouble filling in its left and right edges when not taking in vast horizontal expanses of territory.

Early filmmakers tried **masking**—cropping sides or top and bottom of an image by blackening them out—to achieve more representative verticals and horizontals; however, attempts to fool the screen's rectangle have met with little success. But limitations are the teething rings of art, and the inherent limitations of a horizontal rectangle force a filmmaker to compose a scene carefully and, when he needs more or less space than the rectangle provides, to take the viewer psychologically beyond the confines of the frame or to use objects to restrict what can be seen (making a wall, a tree, or even a head into a masking device). Thus an apparent limitation can become a positive force, in much the same way that the tight rhyme scheme of a sonnet becomes a constructive challenge to a poet.

One fortunate aspect of film composition is that a filmmaker can, by implication, extend the range of the frame. A frame of the bottom half of the Eiffel Tower seems to keep rising, and the viewer senses upward motion. An upward sweep of the camera further enhances a sense of rising movement. The feeling that "there is more there" has direct counterparts in prose. A **synecdoche,** for example, is a figure of speech that uses a part to signify the whole ("ten hands" means ten workmen, a "set of wheels" means a car, and so on). The viewer of a film need only see a periscope to recognize "submarine" or a hand to be aware of "person." The whole need not be seen to be realized. This reliance on parts allows a filmmaker psychologically to extend the frame. A viewer senses great lateral movement when a hand and arm cross the screen because he is aware that the hand and arm are attached to a person. Through a viewer's ability to imagine—to read images not in a literal and dissected way—a film can transcend its physical limits.

Unlike the human eye, the camera sees indiscriminately. Everything in its view will be recorded. Consequently, the relationships between foreground and background are extremely important. Depending on how a filmmaker places objects, they can either divert or attract attention. If a man's face, for example, fills the right one-third of a screen just before the marshal draws in a gun fight, the face either blocks out part of the action to lead the eye to what will happen, or the face provides a response to what is happening, becoming central for an instant. If the former is intended, the face will be either slightly or completely out of focus; if the latter is intended, the face will be completely in focus, while the marshal will be out of focus or in focus less sharply than the face. The director consciously leads the viewer's eyes to where they will perceive the most significant details.

COMPOSITION IN MOTION

Since film depends on motion, the movement of people and objects within the frame is as important an element of composition as the way people and objects line up originally. Unlike still photography or painting, composition within the frame of a film changes with each movement. Each change affects the viewer's perception of an image. Since film has boundaries on four sides but none in depth except that determined by a filmmaker, most effective movement occurs at least in part toward and away from the camera. Unless handled carefully, vertical and horizontal movements of characters remind the viewer of the limits of film's dimensions.

Movement toward and away from the eye, however, creates a sense of depth and of the viewer's involvement in what occurs. Movement toward the camera generally intensifies action and creates a sense that something significant is about to happen. Movement away from the camera appears wistful and serious. Cross-screen movement always seems much more rapid than depth movement, creating a feeling of excitement, but frequently at the expense of a sense of direction and purpose. Depth movement, on the other hand, normally displays significant content, while cross-screen movement creates flurry and action.

The movement of the frame itself also contributes significantly to the total feel of cinematic composition. Not only does the frame move from shot to shot by alternating among close-ups, mid-shots, and long-shots, but the frame also has the capacity to move during a shot. If the marshal chases outlaws from right to left, the frame will follow them by panning. A **pan** is used either to follow a horizontal action or to sweep across a stationary scene. A pan occurs when a stationary camera turns horizontally and the viewer sees new areas revealed in movement from right to left or left to right.

If the marshal catches the outlaws and one begins climbing a ladder to escape, the camera would follow by tilting. A **tilt shot** occurs when a stationary camera angles up or down. Pan and tilt shots extend whatever thrusts of movement occur within the frame. In addition, movements within shots have assumed directional meanings by analogy to the map. For example, movement from right to left implies an east-to-west direction (note which way the wagon trains go in the next western you watch).

Other shots are designed to follow motion as well. A **crane shot** is taken from a boom that can move vertically and horizontally at the same time. A **tracking shot** involves a mobile camera that follows the subject by moving on tracks or by being mounted on a vehicle. A **trucking shot** involves any moving shot with the camera on a mobile mounting, although the term best applies to a camera mounted on a truck. The viewer gains a sense of participation and presence when the camera follows action at a constant distance.

Movement toward and away from a subject occurs chiefly during dolly shots and zooms. A **dolly** is a platform on wheels serving as a camera mount capable of movement in any direction. During a **dolly-in,** the camera moves toward the subject; for a **dolly-out,** the camera travels away from the subject. A **zoom** is accomplished with a lens capable of smoothly and continuously changing focal lengths from wide-angle to telephoto. As the lens **zooms in,** the center of composition gradually fills the screen; the center diminishes as the lens **zooms out.**

While dolly and zoom shots resemble each other in their ability to move toward and away from a subject, they differ in effect. Once focus is set on a zoom lens, it need not be reset as the focal length is increased or decreased since the camera-to-subject distance is constant. A dolly shot, on the other hand, changes the relationship between camera and subject, requiring a change in focus and also bringing about a change in the relationship between subject and background. The effect is the difference between walking closer and closer to someone versus looking at him from a distance through increasingly powerful field glasses. Through the glasses, only the size of the subject changes, and that change occurs at the same rate that the background increases or decreases in size. The dolly, on the other hand, provides changing perspectives and consequently a strong sense of movement through space. Usually a dolly involves a relatively small change in the size of the image, while a zoom moves freely from very close to very far away.

Each kind of camera movement is a tool a filmmaker uses to direct the eyes of a viewer in order to make him aware of particular details and how various details relate to each other. Our eyes do not see indiscriminately in life; we look for certain things and unconsciously ignore others. Since the camera sees indiscriminately, however, the director must act as our selector of visual details. He chooses what our minds will see. By selecting and determining all visual components within the frame, the director controls the emotions and thoughts of his audience. Each movement of the camera provides a rhetorical emphasis as well as a statement of content.

CLICHÉD DETAILS

Because cinematic details evoke ideas, a filmmaker must take seriously even the minor visual elements he includes within the frame. Each segment contributes to an effective film. Elements that are "just there" encourage a viewer's attention to roam and lapse. Effective cinema depends upon a director who has carefully thought out ahead of time what elements will best combine to bring out an idea; weak cinema reveals a director who simply uses whatever is at hand. And, as in writing, it is the commonplace and the cliché that are always readily at hand.

Clichés are trite or hackneyed expressions used to explain an idea. Cliché usually receives a great deal of attention in discussions of writing, but movie clichés are no less prevalent than those of writing. How often in movies have we all heard the following lines and watched the corresponding visuals?

"You ride into town for help. I'll hold 'em off as long as I can."
"I don't like it. It's too quiet."

"If we get out of this alive, I'll have to take you in."
"You wouldn't shoot an unarmed man, would you, Marshal?"
"White man has false tongue."

Such phrases in movies function like such clichés of verbal language as "nice as apple pie," "quick as greased lightning," "the bigger they are, the harder they fall," or "loomed on the horizon." Some viewers become justifiably insulted at repeatedly seeing the same native in a grass skirt saying "bwana" to the pith-helmeted white man. The good guy in white clothes riding a white horse is a stale stereotype, as is his bad-guy counterpart wearing black. As expected, the good guy in *Ben Hur* drives a chariot drawn by white horses, while the bad guy commands black horses. Shots taken directly into the sun with all the appropriate lens flares are empty when the shots seem included only for prettiness and add nothing to content. When a hero finds the going tough, why must he assume some sort of Christ pose?

All of these clichés seem obvious enough, but they keep showing up year after year on the screen. They are unfortunately the most easily available means a filmmaker has of saying something. He simply needs to think "western" and a whole series of worn-out characters, phrases, and actions will come tumbling into his mind. But they communicate ineffectively. Overuse has drained their energy. Details must be included in a film because they reveal universal problems in a fresh context. The nature of film's reliance on detail requires avoiding details that by overuse have become trite abstractions.

Yet it must be noted that statements become clichés partly through their context. What is cliché in one instance might not be in another. By controlling context, a filmmaker can effectively energize almost any cinematic formula or convention.

MISE-EN-SCÈNE

Mise-en-scène is a French term filmmakers have adopted for the aura emanating from details of setting, scenery, and staging. In an effective film, such details go beyond decoration or cliché and help reveal ideas and attitudes.

Consider the types of information you learn about a person by going to his home. Messy? Dirty? Nothing out of place? Sterile? Bare walls? Books? Colorful? Paintings? Everything in a person's home tells you something about what a person values. Filmmakers are very conscious of the way individuals express their inner selves by the way they structure and adorn their environment. Both major and minor details are usually more than mere decoration; they reveal aspects of character in a film. In *Citizen Kane,* for example, Orson Welles uses the aging Kane's castle,

Xanadu, to show the man's love of external splendor but his internal coldness and emptiness. The main living room of Xanadu is the size of a ballroom, with a huge walk-in fireplace dominating the setting. Across the distance of the cavernous room, Kane and his wife shout at each other, but their words ring hollowly from the darkened corners. The set helps a viewer sense the hollowness Kane and his wife feel in their souls.

The most exaggerated use of *mise-en-scène* is found in the German expressionists of the 1920s (in the films of such men as Fritz Lang, Robert Weine, G. W. Pabst, and F. W. Murnau). Expressionism uses details of setting primarily to depict the internal state of mind of a character. Twisted rooms with strangely formed windows, for example, reveal insane or deformed minds. Contemporary horror movies carry on many of the techniques developed by the expressionists. The castle of Dracula is always remote, forbidding, dark, decrepit, empty, and mazed with strange twisting corridors and rooms. The settings make the viewer feel Dracula's inner character while providing the atmosphere that stirs the audience's emotions.

Costuming serves a function as significant as setting and location. While clothes are at least partially utilitarian in life, their function is almost exclusively rhetorical in film. Clothes create an image and convey information about a character's personality. Think of Chaplin's hat, shoes, and cane, or Keaton's hat, or the sleek garb of Mrs. Robinson in *The Graduate*. In a formula western, the good cowboys all look pretty much alike, as do the slightly more rumpled bad men. The hero and villain, on the other hand, wear distinctive good-guy and bad-guy clothing. When a man enters town in a western wearing a suit, ruffled shirt, and string tie, the viewer knows the guy is either a pretty-boy gambler or a weak-kneed easterner. And such dress creates audience hostility (viewers are conditioned to relate certain types of clothing to a series of unfavorable character traits) and expectations (of his being shot or of his being reformed).

Like the masks used in the ancient Greek theater, makeup also adds details to character. Masks have been commonplace in the theater for thousands of years. A viewer can see the striking lines of a mask from far away, where normal facial movements would go unnoticed. Although the expressions of masks are immobile, they allow a great variety of emotions and meanings to be communicated at great distances. Film has changed the need for all that. The camera's ability to move in close to a face lets the viewer scrutinize every nuance of expression. Movements of eyes and mouth can be stressed and enhanced through the subtle applications of makeup. Characterization can also be established largely with makeup, as when a face is made hideous with scars or deformities.

Masks do, however, appear occasionally in movies, usually in monster, horror, or science-fiction films. In addition, makeup so heavy that it could be considered a mask appears on occasion when a filmmaker wishes to develop an idea, as in *Marat/Sade* or *Blow-Up*. But in most films, the face itself bears the burden of conveying the details that take the viewer to the depths of a character's soul.

ESTABLISHING AUTHENTICITY

The average fictional film shoots about two-thirds of its footage in a studio. Such an arrangement gives the director a good deal of control over composition, sets, lighting, and working conditions. The detail he works with has been specifically set up to achieve the illusions the director wishes. Ironically, the illusion he usually seeks is one of "reality."

Since the beginning of film, the possibilities of directly recording reality have fascinated both directors and audiences. In the early days of film, people would flock to see scenes they knew well—a railroad train coming into a station, a boat pulling into a dock, or waves washing the shore. The subject made little difference as long as the audience could see motion. Recorded images of mundane reality appeared awe inspiring, especially when projected larger than life.

Once recorded on film, the commonplace became spectacle. Although audiences today demand complexities of plot and character, an element of fascination with film's ability simply to record remains. Consider the delight of most people in their home movies and snapshots. Most are esthetically awful, as those who take them readily admit. Yet there is delight in recording a piece of the commonplace of a person's own life— a child just learning to walk, a baby sleeping in his crib, grandma walking in her yard, a family game of touch football, a picnic in the back yard, lying in the sun at the lake, or a first car.

The process of recording on film transforms and adds magical qualities to what is commonplace in a person's life. Others might not be as enthralled as we are by our pictures, but who fails to get excited over his own photography? Just as words seem to have magical powers in and of themselves, so do photographic images. In a sense they do capture something of our souls, as those in some cultures (who refuse to have their pictures taken) fear.

The same delight in recording mundane reality reveals itself when we see a location we know in a film or when we see a film being made. Recognizing the familiar in a film heightens the sense of its reality. If one has walked by "that building" or sat by "that fountain," a film's illusion of reality has that much more meaning.

Playing upon our delight in identification with the familiar is part of the rhetorical stock-in-trade of the filmmaker. He knows that we will believe the familiar, and that by creating an atmosphere of familiarity he is more likely to convince us to accept his other offerings. To ease the process of adding the familiar to a film, large libraries are maintained with what is called library or stock shots or footage. **Library** or **stock shots** include any shot not taken for a particular film but used in it. The large libraries of stock shots provide footage that is used so often that there would be no reason to shoot it each time—and such footage helps cut the costs of filming. For example, how often in movies do you see shots of jets taking off, flying, and landing? Such shots are very "real" to most people since most of us have either flown in the same jets or watched them take off and land. The director uses this common aspect of personal experience to establish the reality of his story line as well as to suggest the travel and time relationships occurring within a film.

Even if a viewer has not been to a particular place, he frequently feels he "knows" a location by having seen certain stock footage many times. How many times in films have we seen Trafalgar Square or Piccadilly Circus in London, complete with red double-decker buses? The Trevi fountain and the Colosseum in Rome? The Empire State Building and skyline of New York City? The Eiffel Tower and Arch of Triumph of Paris? The cable cars going up and down the steep hills of San Francisco? Though most people have not visited these places, they are as "real" when seen on film as the maze of freeways and traffic jams most of us are used to. If a viewer looks closely at a film he will be surprised at how many shots are included of things he knows from the constant exposure of direct and indirect experience. Any detail taken from shared experience convinces more readily than what is genuinely strange.

Even when establishing shots (any shot that "establishes" where action is located) or library footage are not familiar, they can create a sense of reality. For example, *Casablanca* (starring Humphrey Bogart) opens with an establishing shot of the entire city of Casablanca. The shot, which is not repeated during the film, might have been recorded by filming a painting, an old or new photograph, or actually taken for the movie from an airplane or high hill near the city. Or, the picture might be of some other city, and few people would know the difference since Casablanca is not on the usual tourist routes. Since World War II was in progress when the film was made, it is highly unlikely that a picture of the city was actually taken for the film. But the "genuineness" of the picture makes no difference. The opening shot provides psychological orientation, and that is enough "reality" for the director's purpose.

Some films adapt segments of real events or things in an even more significant way. Consider, for example, a film using real riot scenes as part of a story about two lovers or about an alienated youth. (Indeed, some filmmakers went to the 1968 Democratic national convention in Chicago to get such footage for their stories and included their actors in the actual riots.) Films based on real incidents use evidence from reality in much the same way. Real events are restaged and the fictitious action captured on film. (*Potemkin, The Battle of Algiers,* and *Z* are notable examples of restaged historical events.) A film such as *Citizen Kane* uses a viewer's expectations of apparently recorded reality by including near the beginning a newsreel that is fictitious but appears genuine. Mixing fictional detail with real, or apparently real, detail enhances the sense of total reality and blurs the distinction between "real" and "fictional."

THE PERSUASIVENESS OF REAL DETAILS

Creating a sense of the presence of recorded reality provides film with its most persuasive powers. A filmed record seems to be a piece of irrefutable evidence because we "see it with our own eyes." We respond as if pictures cannot lie even though we know intellectually that isn't so. This occurs partly because film works immediately upon the senses. A film must captivate the senses, as well as the intellect, to be successful. The emotional logic of a film moves the viewer along at the same time that the logic of argument works. From the multitude of film details we continually draw conscious and unconscious conclusions.

It is the *sense* of recorded reality, not the genuineness of it, that makes film believable and causes a viewer to accept the relationships among photographed details. Raw reality is never seen; even if a camera is left running, a viewer is bound to what the cameraman chooses to include within the bounds of the frame, the closeness with which he photographs what happens, the angle from which he observes, the volume and method of sound reproduction, and so on. In most cases, greater distortion results from trying simply to record reality than occurs from encapsulating it. By editing out irrelevancies captured by the camera, the filmmaker can present major events and their impact. Frequently people who have been involved in an event know little about the most significant aspects until they see the event as someone has recorded it.[2]

Few filmmakers waste time trying to capture any convenient piece of reality that happens along. Instead, they will look for images of great intensity that can be assembled to produce an idea or feeling. The most effective images do not work on the verbal level. For example, a filmmaker can quickly evoke feelings of sadness and disgust by showing hunters clubbing to death helpless white baby seals. The idea of the brutality of slaughtering helpless baby seals can emerge from as little as a single shot.

A filmmaker does not usually include shots simply because they show action. Although cinema depends on movement to involve the viewer,

---

[2] *Gimme Shelter,* the Maysles brothers film of the Rolling Stones' Altamont concert, is a good example. Most spectators at the actual event had no more specific knowledge about the violence and murder that occurred than those who stayed home.

movement without meaning is seldom effective. (The chief exceptions occur in experimental films exploring the esthetics of form and movement.) Most shots in a film attempt to present an idea or feeling. The image of a helpless baby seal being clubbed to death provokes both an emotional and a moral response when included in the proper context. In this sense, a single shot functions much like a model paragraph containing a single controlling idea, clarification of the idea, and evidence in support. A film cannot verbally say "this shot shows rejection, this one love, and that one friendliness"; but shots convey the same meanings by effectively presenting their own details. Consequently, the "image" of a shot is both abstract and concrete. Out of the image grows a general statement, yet the shot usually supports its own argument.

The dual load of conveying detail and idea prevents the image from being a record of raw reality. Instead a shot *represents* some aspect of reality, both re-presenting (presenting again) and symbolizing (standing for something else). The recorded image is simultaneously both a re-creation and a likeness portraying something. A filmmaker chooses an image to represent his point. The hungry girl in a tattered dress with a chocolate cookie sitting among children with hot lunches is both a hungry girl and an image portraying why Senator Mondale thinks our system's response to hunger is a disgrace. Film images are sensuously apprehended details, but each detail—if effective—also serves as a symbol, a thought-bearing image conveying complex associations.

A filmmaker normally includes an image not because it is pretty, but because it makes a point. If a filmmaker were to make a full-fledged documentary about hungry children in the schools, he would probably not include shots of steamboats on the Mississippi. Images of steamboats are very interesting, but they do nothing to further a point about hungry children. The filmmaker might choose to include shots of students working in a classroom, but such shots, no matter how exciting, would be worthwhile only if they related to or represented something about a child's hunger from not receiving proper food.

Most films begin with a clear sense of purpose, just as most written essays operate with a definite goal in mind. Both writer and filmmaker want to say something to somebody. Communication begins with intent. If the purpose of a fiction film is to show the psychological makeup of a character, the film will be written and directed with images developing that purpose, much as a novel will reveal character. By constructing a situation and showing how a character responds, both filmmaker and novelist convey aspects of character to the viewer or reader.

We can see, then, that ideas and details are inextricable in an effective film. The impact of an idea originates in the concreteness of a striking visual (or sometimes aural) image, yet the image makes a statement in itself and in the context of other shots, scenes, and sequences. Film states and proves by showing a piece of apparent reality that the film-maker has specifically selected to make his point. The filmmaker's visual method is not statistical, nor abstract, nor based primarily on logic; instead, his method is rhetorical. He selects images because they will stir the imagination of the viewer, and by stimulating the human mind the filmmaker transmits the concepts within his own mind to the mind of the viewer.

DOCUMENTING THE WORLD: SOUND

Although film is primarily a visual medium, visual images are not the only conveyors of ideas and details. Sound also contributes to the way ideas and details reach a viewer.

Even though sound came late and film had to begin as an exclusively visual medium, the nonsilence of the silent film must be recognized. Viewers in the early theaters seldom knew actual silence during a movie since most early films came complete with musical scores for a piano and accompanying instruments. Musical accompaniment muffled interfering noises and welded an audience together by providing dominant sounds for the ear and a guide to appropriate responses to screen action. Even if silence were possible it would seldom have been desirable. Complete silence would have drained away much of the rhetorical effectiveness of a film's visuals. An absence of sound tends to make viewers highly conscious of the small noises running through any audience—coughs, sneezes, shuffling feet, crunching popcorn, guffaws, or wisecracks.

In 1927, however, several minutes of crooning by Al Jolson in the otherwise silent *The Jazz Singer* signaled an end to the silent era. By 1929, the "talkies" were ascendant and silents became almost non-existent on the commercial film circuits.

The invention of an actual sound track both provided enormous practical advantages and changed the creative potentials of cinema. Theater operators no longer had to depend upon often capricious musicians, and a filmmaker could be certain that audiences would hear the same music he intended for the film. But sound strengthened the visuals as well by eliminating the need for titles. Jarring breaks in the middle of powerful scenes could be eliminated. The words on a heroine's lips could now be heard, and captions explaining a situation could be dropped. As the villain tied the heroine to the tracks, every "Help, save me!" no longer needed spelling out, nor did the explanation that the train was due at 5:30. The coming of the age of sound allowed the pace of visual images to increase manyfold and freed the visual image from the burdens of written language. The image could simply be an image.

SOUND TERMINOLOGY

The sounds contributing to motion pictures can be divided into three categories: spoken language, music, and ambient sounds (those contributing to the atmosphere or forming part of the natural surroundings).

Spoken language appears in two forms: dialogue and narration. If a character is visible (or assumed to be just beyond the limits of the frame) the words spoken are **dialogue**. Although written specifically for an audience, dialogue is spoken as if no public audience were present. The speaker aims his words at other characters or simply talks out loud to himself in soliloquy. He appears unaware that a public audience overhears his every word. As a viewer experiences a film he becomes a voyeur looking it on the private lives of people and overhearing their personal conversations.

Narration, on the other hand, is spoken language specifically directed to a theater audience. A voice addresses the audience, providing information necessary to understand a film's message. Technically, a narrating voice takes two forms: a **narrator**, who is either a character in a film or directly involved in its events, consequently representing a particular point of view; and a **commentator**, who is an omniscient source of supposedly unbiased information. The narrator appears most frequently in fiction films, and the commentator provides the explanatory voice of most documentary and educational films.

A commentator normally takes care to make his voice sound objective and trustworthy, while a narrator's personal involvement appears to color his perception of events, frequently producing various tones of voice depending on his emotional state. Hence, a viewer must question the reliability of what a narrator says since he has a personal interest in the events he describes. In some cases, a narrator will say one thing while the visual images of the film will tell viewers that the truth is considerably different from what he thinks it is. The result is dramatic irony. For example, a narrator might explain that the girl he is with loves him passionately, while the viewer sees that she obviously dislikes him. Cinema has only begun to explore the dramatic potentials of revealing a narrator's spoken perceptions and thoughts at odds with reality as recorded visually. (The problems of narrative point of view are examined in further detail in Chapter 4, "Point of View.")

Any spoken language not seeming to come from images on the screen is called **voice-over**. Sometimes, a narrator or commentator will appear on screen, but most narration is voice-over. Occasionally dialogue becomes voice-over by not synchronizing with the visual image it accompanies.

Music also has two forms: *local* and *background*. As with dialogue and narration, local and background music can be distinguished by their relationship to both scene and spectator. **Local music** originates in the scene itself and can be heard by the characters in the film as well as by the audience. An orchestra at an opera or a jukebox in a tavern provides local music. A good deal of information about a character's personality can be suggested by local music. The music a person listens to tells something about him, much as the visual images of his living quarters reveal personality. Local music also adds credibility to a scene. For example, a saloon with our favorite marshal about to have a gunfight with the bad man would be incomplete without a honky-tonk piano playing—stopping of course to signal a change of atmosphere as the two men face each other.

Background music functions much like narration. It "tells" us how to respond to a film's visuals but has no source identifiable within the film. Background music heightens the dramatic impact of a film in several ways. In many films a musical theme resurges throughout in order to create various attitudes in the viewer and to signal particular moods (recall, for example, some of the better-known sound tracks, such as those from *Love Story, A Man and a Woman,* or *Dr. Zhivago*). Background music also provides a sense of locale (especially for westerns), signals the passage of time, anticipates what is to come by echoing foreboding or romantic strains, and establishes and maintains moods. In older movies, background music even identifies character qualities—sinister music signals the villain, while sweet sounds accompany the hero and heroine. While background music heightens the emotional force of a film's visuals, music is most effective when it does not obtrude or become obvious. Dominant music can easily drain the vitality from a film.

Ambient sound includes all nonverbal and nonmusical sounds contributing to a film. Ambient sounds are noises naturally accompanying a scene, such as frogs croaking at a lake, dogs barking at night, a plane's wheels touching ground, footfalls on a gravel walk, a door slamming shut, wind blowing through trees, or an owl hooting at midnight. The number of different background noises is almost limitless.

The sources of ambient sounds need not be, and usually are not, seen. In life, the source of most sounds remains unseen even though we usually know the source and could probably see it if we wished. The wind blowing through trees or a dog barking in the distance lose none of their immediacy by being heard and not seen.

Ambient sounds work much like background music in intensifying mood. A coyote howling at the moon brings feelings of loneliness, and the sudden roar of a car engine creates apprehension. Ambient noises strengthen the feeling of reality created by visual images and make the viewer mentally extend the limits of the frame.

Two elements of ambient sound deserve special mention: **artificial sound** and **silence**. Artificial sound is created synthetically, usually with electronic instruments or by techniques such as playing tapes backwards. It shows up most frequently in experimental films or in films about science fiction or altered states of consciousness. **Silence**, on the other hand, is effective only as a hiatus in the presence of sound. When all sound ceases, silence creates strong moods if set in the proper context. In a chase through a forest, for example, silence heightens fear and anticipation; in a love scene it intensifies the romantic atmosphere. Anyone who has seen one of Hitchcock's thrillers knows how silence can arouse intense emotions.

Producing the final sound track of a film is a matter of patching together a variety of sounds in a process called the **mix**. Spoken language, music, and ambient sound must all be coordinated with visual images. Music and ambient sound are not alone in being added to the sound track in the laboratory. It is quite common for dialogue to be recorded and then dubbed in after all visuals have been filmed.

Dubbing, the process of matching voice with the lip movements of an actor on the screen (also called **lip sync**), offers the filmmaker several advantages. Since all sound can be added later, the normal noise on a set can be ignored, allowing the filmmaker to work in faster, easier conditions. A breeze through trees or across a microphone, a cough, or a dropped glass will not interfere with filming and cause numerous retakes. Actors can concentrate most of their attention on expression, achieving proper voice inflection later, in the studio. Voices may even be substituted in certain cases, as when singing is required of an actor or actress with salty tonsils. (Frederico Fellini, for example, almost invariably substitutes the voices in his films.) The laboratory allows all sounds to be controlled, creating a cleaner sound track and more convincing delivery of lines than is frequently possible with sound recorded on location.

THE USES OF SOUND

Much film criticism focuses on whether sound matters at all. Some critics, especially during the early days of sound, have postulated that only visuals matter and that the less sound there is in a movie the better it will be. The wretched use of sound in the early years gives some support to the opponents of sound. But filmmakers eventually discovered that sound itself was not to blame, but rather the unimaginative handling of its potentials. As filmmakers discovered more about handling sound, it became a positive and creative force in film.

When used effectively, sound does not simply act as a filler or a source of controllable noise. It does more than provide an audial sense of continuity while visual images do their work. Effective sound creates **audial images**. While "image" is usually considered as a visual representation, an image need not be visual. Audial images work upon the mind much as visual images do. The word "image" has its roots in words meaning "to imitate" or "copy." A sound in film both re-presents and portrays. Like visual images in film, audial images do not simply record reality. By choosing to include certain sounds, the filmmaker endows them with more freight than they would carry in life. Consider, for example, a scene portraying a frightened woman, whose life has been threatened, alone in a house. As she sits in a chair trying to knit, she hears the stairway creak. The sound will evoke in her mind, and the viewer's, thoughts of an intruder. The sound is both sensory and the embodiment of an idea, functioning almost identically to a visual image.

Some audial images are so strong that a film's visuals work in support of a sound, contrary to usual film practice. For example, as part of a transitional scene in *Citizen Kane* a screeching bird is heard and then seen flying away from immediately in front of the camera. The flight of the bird alone contains an element of dramatic impact, but it is the suddenness of the screeching sound which creates real force in the shot. The sound is abrupt and loud, startling the viewer and forcing him to examine the image's significance. The bird echoes the harsh, shrill voice (and character) of the departing second wife of Charles Foster Kane. As with the creak of the stairs, the audial image of the bird directs both idea and detail to a specific point.

Poorly handled sound simply restates or re-presents what a viewer sees on the screen. By telling something twice, a filmmaker divides a viewer's attention between sight and sound, blunting the effect of both. Sound must either directly or indirectly support what happens visually, but it must give information not found in the visuals. We have all seen documentaries where the commentator states, "The men run to their canoes and shove off after the walrus," as the men do just that; and then the commentator says, "They paddle after the walrus," as they do; followed by, "The lead man readies the harpoon and throws," as he indeed does. Both visuals and narration unnecessarily say the same thing, and the result is less effective than it could be. Hearing the actual sounds of the hunt would be an improvement, but the commentator still has a place. He could have given us information about the significance of the hunt unavailable through visuals. Duplication of modes of telling is rhetorical overkill.

Because sound must say something that visuals cannot say, much effective sound is nonsynchronous. **Synchronous sound** simultaneously combines a visual image with the sounds apparently issuing from it; **nonsynchronous sound**, on the other hand, joins visuals from one source with sounds from another. When characters speak on the screen and a viewer can tell by their lip movements that what they are saying is identical with what he actually hears, the sound is synchronous. This is the most common, and least imaginative, use of sound. Synchronous sound is necessary for film, but does little in itself to extend impact. All significance comes from the meaning inherent in actual statements or sounds coming from their obvious sources, not from the technique of synchronous sound.

Nonsynchronous sound, on the other hand, occurs when sounds do not have their source in the accompanying visual images. This use of sound has limitless potential. Its most basic use occurs when a speaker's voice is heard, but the camera focuses on the person the speaker addresses. Hence, the viewer receives both the speaker's comment, complete with voice inflections, and the reactions of the listener. Other applications of nonsynchronous sound occur when visual and audial images have no natural relationship, as when visuals show a bomber while the audial plays a Gregorian chant, or when visual scenes of a political convention are accompanied by the "baaing" sound of sheep. Nonsynchronous sound **counterpoints** visual components. By yoking apparently dissimilar visual and audial images, a powerful film metaphor can be achieved. Out of the clash of sight and sound comes an idea.

SELECTION AND STRESS

Modern filmmakers have discovered that sound requires the same careful selection as visuals. Effective sound contributes to a film's total message, becoming part of the rhetoric rather than simply acting as filler. A film artist not only has the liberty to select the most appropriate sounds from an environment (as our ears do in reality) but to join any sound with an image if that combination will most effectively make a point. In formulating an idea and conveying it through concrete images, a filmmaker has a free hand in assembling bits and pieces for his own purposes. The final test is whether the filmmaker's rhetoric brings the viewer to understanding.

Selection is a highly conscious process on the artist's part. In life we are also highly selective in our perceptions, but the process largely takes place at a subconscious or barely conscious level. We can read while a radio plays until someone asks how we can read with the radio going. The sound becomes dominant once it enters our conscious minds. Sounds surround us in life, but we notice them only selectively. And for all practical purposes, they do not exist for us unless we perceive them. As you read this, stop for five seconds to listen to the sounds around you that you have not noticed. Film, however, forces us to perceive all sounds it produces—hence the need for careful sound selection by the film-maker. A microphone cannot discriminate among sounds, as can our minds. When a microphone records all sounds within its range, the result often seems artifical and makes us uncomfortable.

Besides selection, a filmmaker has another tool for manipulating sound: **stress**. Not only must decisions be made about which sounds to include, but the relative dominance of those included must also be deter-mined. By increasing and decreasing volume, a filmmaker treats sound much as our minds do. If we notice a sound, it assumes a degree of emphasis; if our minds drift off, that sound becomes muffled, and we may not hear it at all. If our minds could not "control" the volume of sounds, it would be impossible to talk at a party with many conversa-tions going on around us. The volume of sounds in a film conditions us to accept them in their proper perceptual contexts.

An effective film forces our minds to perceive sounds in definite ways by the manner in which they are treated in relation to other sounds or to silence. The squeak on a stairway in a murder mystery, for example, is most effective when it seems very loud and occurs in the midst of silence. Thus, the sound receives great stress. Or, a filmmaker might cause both a character in a film and the viewer to become aware of a sound grad-ually. For example, if a man were lost at sea on a lifeboat, parched and almost unconscious, he would only slowly become aware of the sound of an approaching plane. At first the sound would blend with the noises made by movement of the lifeboat, but gradually the sound would emerge as the character began consciously to hear the plane.

Sound also provides opportunities for subjective awareness of events. For example, a character might decide to walk away from a conversation and wander to the side of a nearby tree. The conversation is still within his range, but, as his mind drifts off, the volume of sound lowers then increases as he again becomes aware of what is being said.

Sound is a key element of film rhetoric. Most effective sound never simply restates the visuals, but rather extends and deepens visual imagery by generating ideas in new ways and adding details that furnish more information than that provided by visuals alone.

RECORDING EVENTS

The distinction between recorded **reality** and **fiction** is extraordinarily flimsy. Camera and sound equipment record whatever audial and visual action occurs within their range, but a succession of choices exercised by a filmmaker transforms raw reality into self-contained units of ideas and examples. The filmmaker subordinates sound and sight to his own purposes and out of his inner vision grows a heightened reality—new, strange, and demanding the viewer's full attention.

In a very real sense, then, a viewer must respond to all audial-visual communication as if it were theater, rhetorically acted out to entertain, inform, and persuade him. The proportions of entertainment, information, and persuasion will vary, of course, but a viewer can expect all three elements to be present.

Even in what seems to be pure reporting, theater frequently dominates. Much of the news filmed for television is set up for the media and news "makers" will cooperatively stage or even restage events for film crews. For example, in 1970 a group called Students for Soviet Jewry arranged a demonstration in front of the Soviet Union's United Nations mission. The usual color of such demonstrations, as well as the potential for violence, brought out the expected array of television journalists. They dutifully recorded the emergence past police lines of the group's leaders and a few followers, and the reading of a protest against treatment of Soviet Jews. After chants of "Let my people go," the leader threw the protest document to the ground and the chanting group exited. But a late-arriving news team realized it had missed a visually and audially striking piece of theater. Following the usual formula for missed TV news, a reporter asked the group to restage its act. With no hesitation, it did.

In situations such as that described above, restaged events are probably no less real than the original. In other cases, restaging creates a fiction with its own existence independent of real events. But such distinctions mean little from an audience member's point of view since he cannot mentally know or psychologically separate what is staged from what is spontaneous. The very presence of cameras indicates some planning, and almost every demonstration in front of cameras is staged to some degree. Participants are usually advised ahead of time to walk in a certain fashion and to keep signs (carefully prepared in advance) pointed toward the cameras. Careful rehearsal also goes into the group leader's presentation. Most groups who use media for their own purposes could (and would) restage their acts as many times as a willing press would record it. Such groups carefully arrange audial and visual images for the greatest rhetorical effect. This sort of theater does not alter the truth of what a group says, but it does affect reports through media and consequently influences the viewer. Those who stage any event, from a Veterans of Foreign Wars parade to a Woman's Liberation rally, consider its treatment by the media, and the viewer can regard much of what he views as "staged" for rhetorical purposes.

Rather than being an evil of the modern world, staged news is a fact viewers must cope with. A group of people in our society has few ways of getting its ideas to the public since those in charge of news control access to the media. By staging news events, most people who want to be heard seem to get their say. But a viewer can learn to maintain critical distance, expecting and making allowance for a certain amount of chicanery in order to be informed.

A documentarist, like a reporter, realizes that neither he nor his equipment is ever "objective." And he knows that even the presence of his camera alters and forms the course of events it records. In filming real events he normally tries to back visuals with auditory information qualifying and expanding what has happened and putting visuals into some sort of perspective. He would be irresponsible to ignore the existence of and need for the choices he makes in presenting and defining his materials. The demands of the medium lead him to use visuals containing the greatest amount of action, but the idea a viewer might receive from action visuals might be false. A riot, for example, can always appear to be the fault of one side or the other by the way it is filmed. Hence, it is the combination of visuals and commentary that provides viewers with understanding and perspective.

Most news is gathered and reported in haste. A viewer can expect a high percentage of misinformation or inaccurate perspective as a direct function of time. The brief amount of time available on a newscast regulates even the depth of coverage. News anchormen are quick to point out that their programs consist of only "headlines" and that the information conveyed in a half-hour news program would not even fill the front page of a newspaper. In fairness, though, it must be noted that while the amount of verbal communication is low in televised news, film news accounts communicate much more visually than verbally. Although news programs rely less on visuals than other TV programming, the visual images of news reports do a good deal to extend the verbal message. Word count alone does not reveal the amount of information related.

DOCUMENTARY

For in-depth information on a factual subject, we must look to documentaries. Those who first created documentaries realized from the outset that their mission demanded far more than simply recording physical reality. They had seen enough meaningless physical reality in nickelodeons and early movie houses. It was obvious in the early stages of filmmaking that pictures of waves breaking on a shore or of a train pulling into a station failed to say much. These early films conveyed little but physical reality; the images sparked few ideas in a viewer's mind. Many filmmakers, whose first concern was with physical reality, soon wanted to move beyond evoking feelings of simple excitement in viewers.

The emergence of the documentary gave more meaning to recorded images of reality. John Grierson, who coined the term "documentary," defined the purpose of the genre as "the creative treatment of actuality." He chose his words well, placing equal stress on subject matter and the rhetorical and artistic manner by which it is handled.

Most writers on documentary agree on its basic traits. The source of materials is life itself since documentary filmmakers assume that the natural materials of a situation are "truer" than staged actions. The scene and story for a documentary must grow out of an environment rather than from fictional sources, and native actors usually appear. In addition, documentary stresses theme rather than plot. A theme expresses definite purpose—an intent to *reveal* something—while a plot implies a series of fictional events centering on imaginery characters and situations. Documentary normally shuns emphasis on a highly individualized story or use of a famous star. The primary reason for not focusing on an individual or an imaginary situation is that documentary directs its attention chiefly at some sort of social analysis. Modern media look at various problems of modern society, considering men in relation to their environment and their social situation. Documentary does not simply report; it examines, explores, and dramatizes experience in order to reveal some point about the reality the filmmaker witnesses.

Early spokesmen for documentary such as John Grierson and Paul Rotha provided documentary with a sense of high purpose. Both men contributed to the strength and direction of the form through their combined focus on social purpose and experimentation. Documentary, they thought, should inform and enlighten rather than entertain. Grierson freely admitted that he had little concern for film as film; it simply offered the most convenient available medium. Grierson became the first man to employ film as a medium of mass communication. Yet he was not so shortsighted that he used film simply to spread information. He perceived that rhetorical and artistic effectiveness and the conveyance of a humane order were intertwined.

Grierson once explained that "in documentary you do not shoot with your head only but also with your stomach muscles."[1] While Grierson's comment applies to all types of film, it has a special aptness for docu-

---

[1] *Grierson on Documentary,* ed. Forsyth Hardy, rev. ed. (Berkeley: University of California Press, 1966), p. 77.

mentary since the nonfictional nature of the form makes it seem much more logical and information dispensing than it in fact is. To describe the purpose of documentary, Grierson preferred the word "propaganda," although by it he meant the convincing and honest spreading of information rather than the contemporary implication of intentional distortion and perversion of truth for selfish ends. For Grierson, as for most contemporary documentary filmmakers, documentary provided a major method of funneling information on complex social problems to large numbers of people. But that information required emotional as well as intellectual input.

Undigested "actuality"—recalling Grierson's definition of "documentary"—would obviously be ineffective for saying anything pertinent about a society. In every medium, interpretation is essential since neither words nor pictures can fully recapture reality. They can only represent aspects of it. Film, on the other hand, offers stronger possibilities of accurate observation than does any other medium. The viewer can see much of what the filmmaker originally saw. A filmmaker's task is to give form to what the viewer's eyes will see and to be sure images are set in such a way that the human imagination will be able to comprehend and then respond to what is viewed.

To treat actuality creatively, a filmmaker must first capture the essence of an event or condition with visual images and then arrange those images so that they will work upon the viewer's mind in an ordered, systematic way. It matters little whether the filmmaker must arrange his materials or participants ("actors") in a particular way in order to record actuality on film. The viewer seldom detects such manipulation since the filmmaker establishes "naturalness" as a matter of course. The viewer can, however, look for manipulation and ask questions about its effects. Robert Flaherty put a high value on capturing the actions and spirits of distant cultures, but he staged many of the scenes from *Nanook of the North* (one of the most famous documentaries ever filmed) in order to represent faithfully the Eskimo's battle for survival and to provide synthesis to his treatment of the Eskimo's life. The staged events would have occurred of their own accord, but during times and conditions impossible to film.

A documentary filmmaker must frequently tell someone to hoe ground or bake bread at a time or place when the task normally would not be done. If such staging reproduces what the subject would do anyway at another suitable time or place, then the action faithfully represents the reality of the subject. Indeed, not to do such staging at the price of comprehensiveness and meaning would only distort the truth of a film and destroy its credibility.

A documentary normally makes its point and achieves unity by photographing the actions of real people in specific places, but other methods are available as well. For instance, some important documentaries, such as Alain Resnais' *Night and Fog,* use library footage or stills to make their point. In the case of *Night and Fog,* Resnais shows the horror and degradation of the World War II Nazi concentration camps with both still and moving pictures taken by German and Allied photographers in various camps during and immediately after the war. The result is one of the most wrenching experiences a viewer can undergo. Resnais carefully unites photographic materials taken over a period of time by various people and builds the visuals into an overpowering moral statement against the mentality and forces that create and carry out the barbarisms of concentration camps. Almost any method, including those of fictional film, has potential application to documentary so long as the method effectively reveals the subject.

The documentary filmmaker's quest for authenticity and the effective capturing of reality inspired a new documentary style in the 1960s: **cinéma vérité.** Films made in this style look something like the old candid camera record of people's actions. Handheld cameras, natural sound (with little attempt at controlling volume and a great deal of obtruding noise and static), grainy, high-contrast black-and-white film, and the appearance of no rehearsal and only basic editing are the chief techniques. The handheld camera weaves and bobs with the cameraman's movements, creating the effect of being on the spot with a reporter. The impetus for the style came from television news coverage. However, fiction films occasionally experiment with the style, although it is chiefly the province of the documentary. The prime goal of *cinéma vérité* is veracity; the filmmaker wants to convey the illusion that he is showing the whole truth. The effect is rhetorically convincing, although sometimes tedious.

FICTION AND THE DOCUMENTARY FORM

Although a distinguishing mark of documentary is its reliance on actuality, fiction films frequently share this characteristic. A viewer often has difficulty distinguishing a documentary record from a reconstruction or complete fabrication, especially when a filmmaker tries to effect a newsreel or *cinéma vérité* look. Many people who see *The Battle of Algiers* (a reconstruction of the Algerian fight for independence), for example, think that the film uses documentary footage, despite a disclaimer at the film's beginning. The footage used in the film seems so real in showing the Algerian revolution that existing newsreel of the revolution probably looks like footage from the film and could be added to the fictional version.

Since the viewer frequently cannot distinguish documentary from a filmed record of a restaged event or a completely fictional incident, the

line between documentary and fictional film is very thin. Most revolutions cannot be captured on film, but filmmakers frequently reconstruct
revolutions by filming in a documentary style. Are such films still documentaries? Is the use of actual events to be the chief criterion? If so, at
what point does staging make a film fictional? Reaching final answers
to such questions is not possible unless one wants to confine artistic
forms pedantically. When doubts arise about the genre of a film, one
can only point out genre characteristics and avoid treating forms nar-
rowly.

The essay—the nearest print counterpart to documentary—shares
many of the problems of definition faced by the documentary. Essays
appear in many forms, including poems and imaginative stories, and,
occasionally, what at first appear to be essays sometimes turn out to be
guises for fictional presentations.

Because both essays and documentaries do similar things and appear
in many forms, some of the traits shared by the two throw light on each
other. Perhaps most important, both essay and documentary have a
single controlling "voice" examining a restricted topic. As in every
rhetorical situation, that voice operates with a clearly defined attitude
toward its subject (what Grierson calls theme) and a definite tone in relation to its audience. A filmmaker or essayist might orient his materials
to corporation executives in some cases, the intelligentsia or blue-collar
workers in others. Both essayists and filmmakers normally must rely on
evidence that appears to come from real events and people. Statistics,
facts, visualization of events and created examples are standard for both.
Almost all possible sources of evidence can be exploited in support of a
governing idea as an essayist or documentarist sets out to prove a point
or investigate a subject. Most essays and documentaries even use the
refutatio of classical oratory, presenting the opposition's arguments and
then whittling them down.

The great number of short films made during the 1960s focusing
on social conditions provide many examples of films structured on the
same principles teachers of writing generally urge upon their students.
For example, Donald MacDonald's The Season (a fifteen-minute UCLA
student film shown several times on commercial television) displays the
evils of the commercialization of Christmas. After a short and engrossing
introduction, the film makes its thesis clear both audially and visually,
and then sets out to prove it in several sequences constructed very much
like the paragraphs of conventional student essays. One sequence reveals
the exploitation of Santa Claus mythology by showing the leader of a
rent-a-Santa service crassly explaining how his operation works. Another
sequence shows the indifference (indeed, connivance) of the clergy
through an interview with a talkative minister. A third sequence shows
the perversion of the meaning of the traditional Christmas tree by inter-

viewing a Christmas-tree salesman who boasts of bringing the people onto his lot with his pink, orange, purple, red, and even black Christmas trees. The essay format of *The Season,* with its systematic examination of how the various traditions of Christmas are exploited, creates a powerful denunciation of the way, as one character in the film puts it, "Christmas today in the U.S. means making a buck."

Film, however, usually works much more powerfully on the emotions than the essay. Documentaries can propound their ideas by working on the senses while they also work on the intellect. Consider the two paragraphs about hunger in America quoted at the beginning of Chapter 2. The second paragraph creates intellectual response by mentioning the statistics of hunger, but emotional response is difficult since the problem is put in such abstract terms. The first paragraph allows greater depth of response because an image is drawn of a single hungry child with a filthy dress and a chocolate cookie. However, imagine a film showing an actual hungry or starving girl. When such a human figure appears on film, the camera forces the viewer to see torment on the person's face and pain in her eyes. Film quickly gives the viewer the feeling that he is in the presence of irrefutable evidence, and this evidence works simultaneously on emotions and intellect. While a reader can skip over or fail to imagine emotionally troubling scenes, the viewer has difficulty averting either his eyes or feelings.

Film communicates the bulk of intellectual content through sound, and consequently documentaries are more dependent on sound than other film genres. The camera sees only the concrete and particular, while the sound track encourages the abstracting activities of verbal language. While the image of a starving girl, for example, plays on the screen, the voice of a commentator can tell the viewer that "the U.S. has six percent of the world's population and about half the world's resources but an income distribution . . . that awards 77 percent of total income to the top half of the population and only 23 percent to the lower half."

While a commentator directly states many of the ideas propounded in a documentary, he only implies others. This leaves visuals free to convey many ideas in film terms. If people and animals show easily observable signs of being crippled from mercury poisoning, for example, a narrator need not repeat over and over that mercury is harmful and has seriously crippled them. Visual images will do the job more effectively. Explaining that a certain area has an extraordinarily high concentration of mercury in its water and that the people eat fish from this water is sufficient commentary when coupled with visuals showing cats with malformed legs or children who cannot see. The commentator can buttress the visuals with statistics or information, but if he searches for words to portray his visuals, he can overstate and damage his point.

In many ways, documentary film is a major link between visual and verbal communication since at its best it uses both modes of communication to do what they are best at. Sound reveals abstract information through verbal language, while visuals provide energy and detail. An effective documentary seeks to make a point, and it does so by a rhetorically effective presentation of sight and sound. By rephrasing actuality and by presenting reality in a distilled form in relation to a point, documentaries succeed in taking the blindfold and ear plugs from a viewer and forcing him to see and hear the realities both far away and nearby.

POINT OF VIEW

VOICE AND CONTROLLING CONSCIOUSNESS

Few tasks can be more difficult than sorting truth from eyewitness accounts of dramatic events. Frequently the witnesses seem to be describing different occurrences, yet each witness claims that his version is correct. So common are discrepancies in eyewitness stories that attorneys suspect perjury when statements of different people match too closely. Human minds obviously work in different channels, with circumstances and preconceptions conditioning the way each person sees things happen.

When writing we consciously or unconsciously assume a certain role colored by our perceptions, background, and purposes. The role we project when communicating with others is called **voice**. Every time we speak or write we do so with a certain type of voice. Sometimes we speak or write in a calm, assured way; at other times we are nervous, garbling words and phrases. Depending upon our situations, we take on factual, professional voices, questioning voices, the voices of son, daughter, brother, sister, friend, confidant, teacher, salesclerk, and so on. Seldom would we consider using the same voice for different types of audiences. Imagine a mother's shock if she found her son writing to her in the same way he would write to his girlfriend.

51

At times people even assume voices far different from those they see as part of their personalities. For instance, if a person supports a tax increase to construct a playfield for local children, he might write a letter to the local newspaper (probably under a pseudonym) seeming to criticize the plans for the playfield by saying such things as "who cares about the children anyway?" or "let them take their chances in the street!" or "so what if three children were hit last year in our community?" Since the intention of such a voice would be to make the audience react *against* what is said, the voice would be ironic. The intentions expressed by the voice are at odds with the real purposes of the writer.

Voice and writer or speaker are obviously not interchangeable entities. A writer or speaker takes on a different voice each time he transmits a message. Behind every communication is a single controlling consciousness using one or more voices while shaping and altering materials in light of its purposes. The **controlling consciousness** is the mental framework determining the nature and direction of a work, while **voice** is the outward manifestation of the ideas of the controlling consciousness. The absence of a single controlling consciousness—usually one person, but sometimes several minds in agreement—and the failure to project voice distinctly will cause muddled communication.

Not enough attention has been paid to the controlling consciousness, or use of voice, in film. Because film records reality more directly than any other communicative or artistic medium, the viewer can easily assume unconsciously that the filmmaker is showing either reality or a reasonable replica and that therefore no one is subordinating observable details to some purpose. Although a good filmmaker is a trained observer, he and his camera are not necessarily wholly reliable witnesses or evaluators. Most filmmakers try to be honest, recognizing their biases, but even the most objective colors his films with his own predilections. Although each photographable scene has an independent existence, it assumes the qualities of an abstraction in the hands of a filmmaker. It contains an idea apart from its concrete existence, and that idea grows from the selection process of the filmmaker's controlling consciousness. Every choice he makes deepens the imprint of his hand upon his subject. The filmmaker manipulates reality, molding disparate materials to contribute to a unified point of view.

A modified version of Aristotle's rhetorical triangle (opposite) will help clarify the operation of point of view in film. The audience receives information from both directions of Aristotle's rhetorical triangle: the dominant mood and flavor directly from the tone the controlling consciousness sets up; and the series of conflicting but finally resolved arguments and viewpoints made clear through attitude and representation.

Since our primary concern is understanding the rhetoric of film

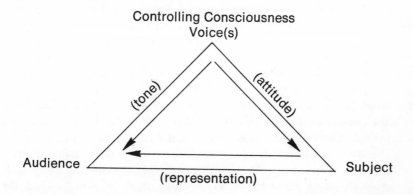

rather than how to make films, the above triangle can be best understood from the **audience's** corner instead of the filmmaker's. The controlling consciousness behind a film speaks to the viewer directly through **tone**. Every film is pitched to move the audience for which it is intended. A tone fitting for grade-school children will not serve for general adult entertainment, nor will a tone appropriate for general adult entertainment fill the needs of sophisticated film buffs.

Tone, however, does not play upon an audience in isolation. Tone allies itself closely with **subject**. A filmmaker does more than convey a particular feeling to an audience. He also has something to say. In a documentary he might focus on starving children; in a love story, on the plight of two lovers when they are faced with the incipient death of one of them; and in a comedy, on the consequences of foolish actions.

An audience perceives a filmmaker's **attitude** toward his subject in a variety of ways. When watching a film a viewer is almost always aware of the many, often conflicting, voices of the major characters. Through these voices the controlling consciousness of a film **represents** a multitude of responses or points of view, letting these play upon his audience. Each voice has its own "tone," which is determined by the controlling consciousness.

The dramatic nature of film requires the interplay of various voices and hence of points of view. Consider, for example, the voices in a hypothetical film. The controlling consciousness wants to show how greed destroys a man and those around him. One voice in the film might be that of a corporation president who has devoted his life to becoming rich. Other voices might include those of his club-oriented wife, their disillusioned hippie son, the son's steadfast and principled girlfriend, and the father's mistress. The filmmaker obviously cannot come on screen for ninety minutes saying that "greed destroys a man." Instead, he sets up many conflicting voices, revealing his theme dramatically. The subject achieves expression not in statement, but through characters and events. Through **representation** the controlling consciousness makes the audience realize his **attitude** toward his subject.

Only in rare instances (usually in documentaries) does the controlling consciousness emerge as the single voice in a film—as it does frequently in poems or essays. Instead, it is by controlling the tensions among various points of view that a filmmaker provides his viewers with a sense of a single consciousness in control. Point of view in film comes from both the dominant **tone** of a work and from the multiple tones provided by **representation** when a subject is handled with dramatic tension.

The dual nature of point of view in film depends on the effective use of a great many cinematic techniques. Before considering more fully the applications of point of view we must review the techniques the filmmaker uses to control and shape the point of view of his characters and ultimately to establish a dominant viewpoint.

THE CAMERA LENS

After centuries of standing in the pit or sitting in far-off balconies, the common man finally found he could sit in fourth-row-center and even walk upon the stage at times for a closer look. From anywhere in the theater, the camera provided a physical relationship to the stage that not even the rich could previously attain. At first, the camera remained in fourth-row-center, providing primarily long- and mid-long-shots. Eventually the camera eye began to roam more freely, extending the rhetorical potentials of film.

Yet, the camera is an instrument not like the human eye. The eye judges depth through stereoscopic vision; the camera does not see in stereo and must rely on setting for the illusion of depth. The eye can instantly adapt itself to a wide variety of changing lighting conditions; the camera cannot. The eye refocuses instantly and unnoticeably, moving at will from objects within inches to those miles away; camera focus is slow and easily seen. The eye has a dominant center of vision, concentrating on certain things while aware of a much larger field (approximately 180 degrees); the camera cannot discriminate among those things that are in focus within the frame. The eye blinks and shuts, closing off the world by accident or choice; the camera keeps running, never blinking or wavering, until the cameraman stops it completely.

Yet these apparent limitations only fuel the art of cinema. Art moves beyond simply recording reality, and instead transforms chance reality into coherence. The supposed limitations of the camera provide and encourage techniques for making statements. An out-of-focus image, for instance, may show a person's mental state. In addition the camera offers advantages of its own. For example, the human body forces the eye to maintain one angle of vision for a long time, yet the camera can be moved to another angle and when two shots are spliced during editing, physical change can occur instantaneously.

The **lens** is the camera's counterpart of the human eye. But unlike the human eye, a camera lens can be changed. By changing lenses, a film-maker can move away from what is normal, rhetorically developing his ideas through a variety of image sizes and perspectives.

Image size can be determined in two ways. First is the **distance** between camera and subject. By moving the camera closer to a subject, its image size will be increased; movement away decreases image size. The second method for determining image size is by **focal length** (literally the distance from the focal point of a lens to the plane of the film, but from a viewer's perspective focal length can be considered the amount of area a lens can photograph from a given distance). A lens with a normal focal length (12 mm for an 8-mm camera, 25 mm for a 16-mm camera, and 50 mm for a 35-mm camera) records an image approximating what the eye sees naturally.

When a filmmaker leaves his camera in the same place but substitutes a lens with a shorter focal length, he will be using a **wide-angle lens**. The wider the angle of vision the lens accepts, the greater the area photographed by the camera. Because a wide-angle lens takes in a greater amount of area than a normal lens, the size of individual objects will be smaller and more difficult to see.

If a filmmaker wishes a lens with a longer than normal focal length, he will use a **long lens** (also called **telephoto**, although technically a telephoto is a lens with greater power of magnification than that of a long lens). A long lens photographs an area smaller than that seen by a normal lens. Thus an object will appear much larger on the screen when photographed through a long lens. (Figures 2a–j.)

Lenses are only occasionally used solely because of distance require-ments. For example, photographing a person across a wide river requires a long lens, while photographing a person in a small room demands a wide-angle lens because the photographer cannot move farther away from his subject. Usually, however, a filmmaker selects a lens for its effect on perspective. **Perspective** is the way objects appear to the eye in terms of their relative positions and distances. A normal lens, of course, provides almost the same perspective as the human eye. But wide-angle and long lenses affect images in often startling ways. Each change in lenses forces the viewer to perceive a shot through slightly different consciousness. The further a lens moves away from what is normal, the more sub-jective the effect.

The wide-angle lens frequently provides more information than a longer lens. More objects appear on the screen, creating a sense of their interrelationships. At the same time, an image seems to be stretched out; objects appear to be farther apart than they are. A hand thrust toward

Fig. 2a. . 35mm camera with a *fish-eye lens* on a 50mm normal lens. Note the distortion caused by this extreme wide-angle lens; the ship in the center is only a speck in the distance, while surrounding buildings dominate.

Fig. 2b.   35mm *wide-angle lens.*

Fig. 2c. 50mm normal lens. This lens approximates what the human eye sees in terms of size and proportion. Note how buildings become less dominant with increasing nearness to the ship.

Fig. 2d.   200mm *long lens.*

photo lens. Along with the increased detail, note how perspective is flattened, making the ship look
than it appears in the other photographs.

Fig. 2f. 20.9mm *fish-eye lens* on a 50mm normal lens. Figures 2f–j show how lenses can alter the relationship between foreground and background. In each instance, the image sizes of the horses and carriages are kept consistent, while the image sizes of the buildings vary greatly. (In Figures 2a–e the photographer stood in the same place, simply changing lenses; in Figures 2f–j he moved further away from the subject with each lens change in order to keep the horses and carriages a similar image size.) Note how the fish-eye lens allows entire buildings to be seen (and distorted).

28mm *wide-angle lens.* This lens cuts off most of the buildings, keeping them deemphasized in the distance. ...gh a certain amount of distortion occurs (the horse seems larger and longer than normal in relationship to ...rriage), the wide-angle lens provides a perspective with great depth.

Fig. 2h. 50mm normal lens. Perspective is approximately what would be experienced by the human eye.

200mm *long lens*. The arched windows in the background begin to look large in relation to the carriages.

Fig. 2j. 600mm *telephoto lens.* The arched windows overwhelm the carriages. Note the change in depth with increasingly long lenses. The 28mm lens reveals great depth while the 600mm lens flattens perspective, making the foreground seem shoved against the background.

the camera will appear huge and out of proportion. In addition, movement toward and away from the camera seems very rapid. Because movement seems so fast, the effect is surprising and frequently threatening, providing an effective vehicle for filming scenes of fighting, arguing, or confusion. Although people seem more isolated and distant when seen through a wide-angle lens than they in fact are, they come together at a startling rate. The ability of the wide-angle lens to exaggerate or emphasize actions or relationships between people provides the controlling consciousness with a ready tool for subjective statement.

The extreme wide-angle lens, called a **fish-eye,** offers the most subjective effect of the wide-angle lenses. Used primarily for scenes of fantasy, drug or alcohol effects, insanity, or dreams, the fish-eye lens distorts everything it sees, creating an eerie sensation. This lens rounds off an image, taking in an immense area with central objects made very prominent.

The **long lens**, or **telephoto**, is much more selective than the wide-angle lens. The long lens compresses space, forcing a subject into its background. A viewer finds his eye guided quickly to key elements as the cameraman selects what is significant from a context. Movement toward and away from the camera seems sluggish and futile. Everyone recalls scenes of actors running hard and appearing to get nowhere; the device has become a cliché now and is especially overused in television ads. The longer the lens, the more ghostly, light, and romantic the effect. While the wide-angle lens is best at providing information, the long lens best conveys mood and emotion by eliminating all but a few key details.

Special anamorphic lenses (which distort through unequal magnification) and prismatic distortions create even further exaggerated effects. The images obtainable from such equipment resemble the grotesque distortions of fun-house mirrors—double or multiple images, bodies appearing fat, elongated, wavy, and so on. Filmmakers use these devices primarily to show great mental aberration.

Wide-angle and long lenses also alter **depth of field** (the range of distances within focus). A wide-angle lens offers great depth of field; objects far away and up close will all be in focus. A long lens, on the other hand, creates a more shallow depth of field. The principal subject will be in focus while foreground and background are blurred, highlighting and concentrating attention on the principal subject.

The more shallow a depth of field, the more segments of an environment are excluded. A great deal of artistic control can be gained by controlling the elements a viewer can perceive. A shallow field, the

The same f-stop setting is named for each lens. The opening and closing of the iris to control the amount of light passing through (as the iris does for the human lens, while an f-stop of 1.4 is "open." The smaller the f-stop, the more light is admitted.

allows **focus-through**, which is a change of field taking the viewer from one object to another previously out of focus. For example, a man will be seen sitting in a car with a frightened look while only a blur can be detected on his far side. Suddenly, the focus changes from the frightened man to another man sitting on the opposite side of the car holding a gun. Focus-through provides an explanation for the look seen in the first shot and forces a reexamination of that shot.

Most lenses can change focus to reveal clear images of objects from a few feet—sometimes inches—to infinity. The cameraman chooses which objects will be in focus by adjusting the lens. Focus gives a filmmaker an additional measure of rhetorical control over where a viewer looks. By blurring segments of background, a filmmaker gives a viewer few alternatives to see. Characters and events can be isolated to control a viewer's responses.

In addition, focus can reveal mental states or moods. A muddled state of consciousness, for instance, can be conveyed by throwing an image (accompanied by slow, distorted sound) out of focus. How many times have we seen a patient wake up through a haze and eventually focus clearly on the worried but reassuring face of a doctor? **Soft focus**, which imparts a hazy but recognizable look to a scene, can also be used in a sustained way to idealize or romanticize a subject. For example, a hero's look at the heroine, a sunset, an old homestead, or a character's return to her home and family after a long absence might be shot with soft focus. Shots out of focus or in soft focus are cinematic defects technically, but, like other apparent cinematic defects, they play upon the surfaces of reality.

Another element associated with the camera lens also provides the filmmaker with control over his materials. **Filters** (transparent glass or gelatin placed in front of or behind a lens) control coloration by either removing certain light waves or making a single color dominant. Light is not homogenous but composed of each of the seven dominant colors of the spectrum. By removing certain light rays, filters allow light properties to be manipulated: Contrast can be increased, a sky darkened, barely visible clouds made striking, or light softened. By using a solid-color filter with colored film, a filmmaker can cause a scene to appear all reddish, bluish, and so on. With other kinds of filters, a "night" scene can be shot in broad daylight yet look like the darkest night on film. In short, filters allow a filmmaker to color and alter reality to fit his own needs. (Figures 4a–d.)

FILM STOCKS AND EXPOSURE

Once an image passes through the lens and shutter (a mechanism allowing light to pass through only briefly), it must be recorded on **film stock**. Light-sensitive **emulsions** record cinematic images on long strips of cellu-

Fig. 3a.   A large *depth of field* created by stopping down to f16 (taken with a 50mm normal lens in a 35mm camera). Note how even distant background is in focus, while the same background in Figure 3b has all texture blurred.

Fig. 3b. A shallow *depth of field* created by opening up the lens to ƒ1.4. Note ·the ability of the lens to select one plum to remain in focus while adjacent fruit remains out of focus.

Fig. 4a.   50mm lens without a filter.

Fig. 4b. A red filter establishes a much darker and more ominous scene, making clouds threatening and throwing the city into murky shadows.

Fig. 4b. A polarizing filter changes the tones of the scene, creating a darker sky and more sharply defined clouds.

Fig. 4d. A yellow filter puts the city in dim shadows with clouds darkened.

loid. Film comes in widths of 8mm (both standard and super eight), 16mm, 35mm (a standard for still photography), and occasionally in 70mm and larger. Everyone knows 8mm from home movies and 16mm from classroom use. Theaters have almost exclusive use of 35mm and larger. As film size increases, so does image quality, allowing crisper images for larger screens. However, the equipment needed to record and project 35mm is too large and expensive for amateurs.

The emulsions on film stocks vary in both light sensitivity and appearance. Stocks called *slow* need more light to record an image than *fast* stock. Slow stock is appropriate for bright, well-lighted conditions, while dim light requires fast stock. An observable difference generally distinguishes the two. Slow film stock offers a more even and polished image than fast stock, which appears grainy and contrasty (as in newspaper photos).

Both shooting conditions and the filmmaker's intentions affect the selection of a film stock. The normal viewer does not consciously notice contrast and granularity, and has no way of knowing a film stock's speed. Yet the viewer has unconscious associations about the way various films appear, and the filmmaker capitalizes on these associations. Fast films were first used in reporting situations requiring natural light. Consequently, the grainy and contrasty effect of fast film connotes on-the-spot recording of events. When a film looks rough and stark it seems more realistic. Both fiction and nonfiction films use this convention to create a spontaneous, unrehearsed quality. While semifast color films exist, for newsreel effect black and white is always the choice. (Figures 5a–d.)

Cost legislated against the wide use of color until recent years, but the price difference between color and black and white is no longer as significant. Filmmakers now choose film stock for its psychological implications rather than for economic reasons. Early use of color, on the other hand, was confined to extravaganzas, musicals, and travelogues. As costs have declined and filmmakers have found ways to manipulate color, many film artists have gradually adapted color to their purposes.

The filmmaker's ability to manipulate is the key to the continued popularity of black and white, as well as to the more recent acceptance of color. The filmmaker seldom cares about simply recording reality; rather he exercises his controlling consciousness on reality, shaping and bringing order. Black and white allows great variety of mood, although color is being used increasingly as it can be altered to fit various moods. Every film stock has rhetorical properties peculiar to it, and it is the peculiarities and their rhetorical applications that interest a filmmaker. It is now common

MOTION PICTURE FORMATS

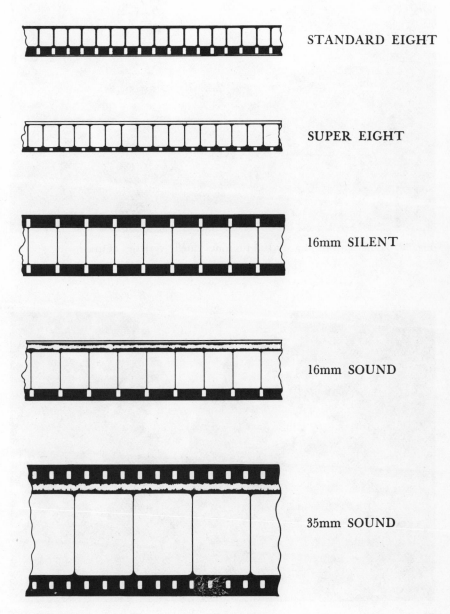

STANDARD EIGHT

SUPER EIGHT

16mm SILENT

16mm SOUND

35mm SOUND

Fig. 5a.   Low contrast film stock, with tones chiefly varieties of gray.

Fig. 5c.   High contrast film stock, moving all tones toward either black or white.

Fig. 5b. Medium contrast film stock, making the scene harsher, sharper, and more grainy.

Fig. 5d. Extremely high contrast (black and white line), revealing only blacks and whites and hence creating a sense of artificiality and coldness.

The rhetorical properties of a film stock can be further enhanced by exposure. Like the eye, the camera has a device (resembling the iris of the human eye) called a diaphragm for controlling the amount of light passing through. By opening and closing the diaphragm (by turning a camera's *f*-stop ring) the brightness of an exposure can be controlled. Overexposed film appears too bright and underexposed film seems too dark. Overexposure tends to wash out details and create glaring white areas on the screen. Underexposure, unlike limited light, does not usually destroy significant details but it does establish a dark and serious atmosphere. (Severe underexposure can, however, destroy details by bleeding out texture.) Such controls provide the filmmaker with yet another way of forcing the viewer to see an image in a particular way.

MANIPULATION WITHIN THE CAMERA

One major method of manipulating within the camera the effect an image will have is **camera speed.** By speeding up or slowing down an image, the rhetorical effect is altered. **Slow motion** has inherent grace. Any subject is romanticized by slowing it down. Hence, filmmakers use slow motion for sweet and romantic scenes and to show dreams or memories. Unlike the ballet sense of fluidity found in slow motion, **fast motion** exaggerates movements, making almost any gesture look clumsy and comic. Because of its comic exaggeration, fast motion became a stock-in-trade technique in such early comedies as those of the Keystone Kops. Actions that were quite safe to perform at normal speed appeared simultaneously dangerous and funny when speeded up. (Early projectionists added to the speed—even in serious films—by trying to crank through as many films as possible in a given time.) Filmmakers employ slow and fast motion only in specific situations now, but the conventions of each still prove extraordinarily effective.

Whether achieved in the camera or in the laboratory, many other devices help establish point of view. **Double exposure,** for example, occurs when two separate images occupy the frame, overlapping and commenting on one another. Double exposure is another device used to show the inner workings of the mind. By showing simultaneously a person's face and his actions in the past, a filmmaker records thought processes or dreams. Double exposure also depicts the supernatural, allowing ghostly figures to move through walls and objects while the viewer sees through the "transparent" bodies.

Another device for showing fantasy is the **negative image.** If a viewer looks through a normal negative for black-and-white prints, he sees the black tones of the print appear white on the negative. By reversing blacks and whites, the filmmaker creates a world where normal tonal values have been reversed. Reality itself appears to be reversed. The result has a variety of effects, primarily distancing the audience and creating a sense of fantasy. (Figure 6a.)

CAMERA PLACEMENT

A filmmaker not only exercises control over the way his camera records, but he manipulates his material through where he puts it as well. The normal height for a camera to be placed—and therefore aimed when level—is slightly below the eye level of a person. Any movement away from this norm alters perspective and has connotations exploited by filmmakers. The most important variations involve movement on the camera's vertical plane. If the camera looks upward, the result is a **low-angle shot**. A low-angle shot sets the subject against the sky or a ceiling, providing the subject with an air of dominance and of being larger than life. The point of view suggested by a low-angle shot is often that of a child, a small person, or someone who feels inferior and who must "look up to" whatever the camera photographs. When the camera is aimed downward, a **high-angle shot** results. The point of view is that of a tall person, and whatever is seen is looked down upon and made to appear weak. The subject is reduced in size and put in the position of an underling.

High- and low-angle shots convey attitude, showing what the subject feels in relation to the people or objects around. Consequently, a filmmaker in part tells the viewer how to feel about a character or an action by shot angle. The greater the angle, the more a feeling is intensified. If, for example, a filmmaker wants an orphan in a poor house to look overwhelmed and powerless (as does David Lean in *Oliver Twist*), the filmmaker would use very low-angle shots to re-create the boy's viewpoint and suggest his feelings of being overwhelmed by a large and hostile world. Decreasing the camera angle would reduce the viewer's sense of the boy's feelings of intimidation. In some cases a filmmaker will use an extreme angle to make a point. An extreme high-angle shot might appear to be directly above the subject, while an extreme low angle will be shot with the camera on or below floor level. (Figures 7a–c.)

Cameras can be held at other angles to enhance various feelings. Occasionally a camera will be placed upside down, for instance, disorienting the viewer and making him uneasy. At times a camera will be angled as if the camera man were leaning left or right. Such angles can also disorient or even create a wavelike movement if continued from side to side. But odd angles most effectively emphasize a condition. By angling the camera to make a hill look steeper, for example, the efforts of a man climbing the hill seem that much more impressive. Emphasizing the steepness for someone moving downhill intensifies the feeling of danger.

Fig. 6a. *Negative image,* reversing reality and distancing the viewer.

Fig. 7a. A standard straight-on shot.

Fig. 7b. A *high-angle shot*, using the camera's point of view to look down on the subject and to show him in a precarious position.

Fig. 7c. A *low-angle shot*, using the camera's point of view to establish the subject's dominance and sense of being "on top of it all." If in an actual movie the high-angle shot of Figure 7b were followed by a low-angle shot of a grim-faced man, the viewer would assume that the point of view was now that of the child looking upward; the man would appear dominating to the point of being intimidating.

Camera angles do not create content, but modify it. They change the composition of shots, using perspective to achieve rhetorical and psychological emphasis. As with other camera devices, the greater the degree of movement away from the norm, the greater is the conveyance of individualized feeling and attitude.

The apparent distance from camera to subject also varies in appropriateness for conveying different attitudes. Length of shots is, of course, a relative matter. If the subject is a herd of moose, a close-up would include the entire herd; if, however, the subject were a particular moose, a close-up might only include the moose's head and horns. Certain types of shots most appropriately dominate certain kinds of films. Love stories or psychological studies require the intimacy of close-ups; documentaries or satires rely upon a predominance of longer shots (especially when characters operate as types rather than as individuals). Close-ups, as Godard once observed, work best for tragedy while comedy depends on long-shots. The close-up best conveys emotion while the long-shot carries facts or relationships. Consider for example a long-shot of a group of men standing outside a courtroom juxtaposed with a close-up of a man's tightened face as he nervously pulls at a cigarette.

Even camera movement helps develop point of view. If a character looks to the right, the camera pans right following his glance and then sees what he sees. If the camera fails to follow his glance, but shows something else in the next shot, the viewer will be confused. Convention requires that after a shot of a person distinctly looking in a direction another shot must show what that person is actually seeing. Every movement of the camera reflects a spontaneous apprehension of detail.

LIGHTING

In the filmmaker's effort to control atmosphere and establish point of view, **lighting** is a key element. Occasionally, local light (an exposed bulb, a blazing neon sign, the row of lights at a football stadium) will contribute to mood because the light source recognizably relates to the subject at hand. But in most cases, a viewer remains unaware of the origin of lighting.

Lighting can be either **natural** (usually from the sun) or **artificial**. The color properties of natural lighting change constantly from the warm reddish cast of sunrise and sunset, or the ominous grayish-green depth preceding a thunderstorm, to the bright, flat, and relatively colorless light of the noontime sun. The intensity of natural light also ranges from the brilliance of noon to the dimness of the long, darkened shadows of evening and the cold, shallow light of the moon.

Artificial lighting, on the other hand, has fixed color properties that are highly predictable and consistent. With artificial lighting the filmmaker can control the effect of lighting over a long period of time. Light intensity contributes heavily to atmosphere and meaning. A sunny day, for instance, conveys feelings of exuberance and joy, while dark days seem depressing and threatening. The increasingly strong light of the rising sun speaks of birth and renewed life, while the flickering rays of the setting sun suggest decline and death. Lighting that puts most of a setting in shadow is called **low key**; **high-key** lighting is bright and relatively shadowless. Low-key lighting heightens suspense and creates feelings of gloom and mystery. Horror movies and most old detective movies rely on low-key lighting. High-key lighting, on the other hand, characterizes comic or happy moods. It is the optimistic and cheerful lighting used in comedies and romances.

In addition to the general lighting of a set, special **lighting angles** also enhance aspects of character. **Front light** generally softens and blurs a face, flattening and taking away character while making a face seem more beautiful. **Side light** creates a sense of depth and solidity while lining a face and detracting from loveliness; side lighting frequently makes a face look mysterious. **Back lighting** idealizes a face, while adding a feeling of depth by separating a subject from its background. **Bottom lighting** produces a sinister, evil appearance. Finally, **top lighting** provides a mood of freshness that often seems spiritualized.[2] Each angle of lighting provides the filmmaker with another rhetorical device to establish point of view. (Figures 8a–e.)

NARRATIVE VOICES

Every film reflects its creator. His style emerges as he colors his materials. A whole school of criticism, basing itself on the *auteur* (French for "author"), has even evolved to glorify the greatest film styles. While the *auteur* theory concentrates perhaps too heavily on one aspect of filmmaking, it does point out that the creation of a film strongly depends on a controlling consciousness. Even though many people contribute to and participate in the cinematic process and although films appear to be made by committees, a single dominant point of view emerges from an effective film. The director usually provides the necessary controlling consciousness.

From the variety of sound and visual techniques open to him, the director selects those best suited for conveying his ideas and attitudes to his audience. He also exercises choice over such matters as actors and locations, making each decision in the light of his ultimate purpose. Since film is a dramatic medium, the director must provide and nurture

[2] Cf. Ralph Stephenson and J. R. Debrix, *The Cinema as Art* (Baltimore: Penguin, 1965), p. 172.

Fig. 8a.   Front lighting (an example of high-key lighting).

Fig. 8b.   Side lighting (an example of low-key lighting).

Fig. 8c.   Back lighting.

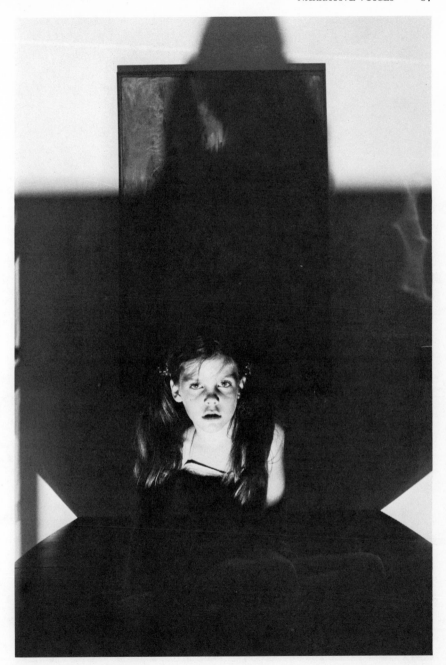

Fig. 8d. Bottom lighting.

Fig. 8e.   Top lighting.

the numerous contradictory voices out of which the unified vision of a film grows. Hence, the filmmaker must determine the range and dominance of narrative voices.

The narrator, of course, is always the camera in one way or another. We see (both literally and figuratively) through its eye. Yet the camera never simply "looks" and sees haphazard reality. The camera "looks" where and in the fashion the director and cameraman cause it to look. Within a single film it is sometimes a neutral observer, sometimes a witness, and sometimes a participant. That is, the controlling consciousness of a film creates a great many points of view and adapts all of them to his purposes. The viewer sees such points of view frequently and unconsciously responds to their effects. The following diagrams (Figures I–IV) will help distinguish among them. Each figure shows the screen as the viewer would see it in different versions of the same shot. In Fig. I, the **camera-as-narrator** (also called the "camera eye" or "fly on the wall"), the camera watches a story unfold, seeming to record what occurs before its lens. The story appears to be revealed in an objective manner; the camera responds like a disinterested third party of fiction who calls people "he" or "she" or "them." The camera-as-narrator is the usual viewpoint in film. It can be used continuously, appearing to reflect reality, and making few mental demands on the viewer. The passive camera seems to be a trustworthy witness, and so the viewer relies upon its apparent omniscience.

But the illusion of objectivity is a rhetorical device exploited by the filmmaker. The camera as an objective narrator is not objective at all, but subject to the controlling consciousness of the filmmaker. An audience thinks it is simply being shown the events of a story, but the filmmaker carefully controls point of view with such things as film stock, lighting, setting, and camera angle. The apparently objective point of view is as subjective as all of the devices used by the filmmaker. Rather than being an objective, disinterested, or reliable narrator, the camera is the tool of the operative point of view of the filmmaker. The camera as witness and the controlling consciousness are one, and the same message moves directly along the triangle from voice to audience and indirectly from voice through subject and on to audience.

In some films the controlling consciousness will capitalize on the camera's familiar but objective quality by addressing an audience directly. For example, in *Tom Jones* the hero winks to the camera, claps his hat over the lens (accusing the audience of voyeurism and insisting on privacy), and in one case creates a **wipe** by closing double sliding doors against the all-seeing camera eye and opening them after a discreet interval. (A **wipe** is a transitional device in which one image slowly replaces another on the screen by pushing the other out of the way). Sometimes a filmmaker will leave in his film a directorial comment

Fig. I. *Camera-as-narrator.* The camera "objectively" witnesses everything.

Fig. II. *Witness-as-narrator.* A witness narrates, and the camera can see him.

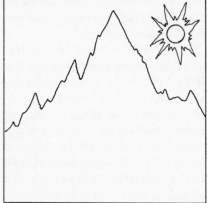

Fig. III. *Protagonist-as-narrator.* The protagonist narrates, but the audience can see him.

Fig. IV. *Subjective camera.* Inside the protagonist's mind.

made during shooting, or some other "mistake," as a way of reminding the viewer that he is watching a film and that he cannot put full trust in the seemingly objective camera. Such efforts help make viewers more critical by reminding them that the controlling hand of the filmmaker is at work.

When a **witness-as-narrator** (Fig. II) appears, a viewer senses a point of view shaping materials according to preconceptions. The viewer becomes "on guard" for point of view. Occasionally a story uses several witnesses-as-narrators, all providing a segment of a story. For example, Orson Welles' *Citizen Kane* shows the life of Charles Foster Kane in basically chronological order, but those who were close to him narrate each segment, and each person displays his own prejudices. Thatcher views Kane in terms of money; Bernstein has a comic, chaotic perspective; Leland speaks as a disillusioned friend, seeing underlying weaknesses and showing how things began well but were destroyed by Kane's own flawed character; Susan Kane, the second wife, speaks as a person who loved without being loved in return and who was forced to submit to Kane's will. All of these scenes are, in fact, contrasted with the "objectivity" of an opening newsreel account of Kane's life.

The witness-as-narrator addresses the audience directly or indirectly, and is at least seen at the beginning or end of a sequence. Usually the audience sees and hears the narrator briefly and then a dissolve leads the audience to a dramatization of what he begins to say. When he says "I want to tell you the story of . . ." and the scene comes on, it looks the same as the camera-as-narrator, but the witness-as-narrator has announced his significance and we cannot help but feel a certain awareness of his point of view.

The **protagonist-as-narrator** (Fig. III) operates much like the witness-as-narrator except that the former tells his own story while the latter tells a story about someone else. The protagonist-as-narrator can be seen by the viewer even though he sometimes speaks to an audience, as would an off-screen narrator, and is a part of all the action he narrates. His actual narrative voice is not, however, necessary. When the camera follows him, the audience is aware that the story comes from his point of view, and the filmmaker usually signals the narrator's point of view much as that of the witness-as-narrator is signaled. Like short stories and novels, films can simultaneously maintain narrators who are both storytellers and participants despite the limitations of film's continuous present tense.

When the camera directly enters the narrator's mind, rather than following him, the filmmaker clearly tells the viewer that he must respond to a subjective state. The **subjective camera** (Fig. IV) becomes the eyes of the protagonist, and consequently viewer, protagonist, and narrator look at identical things. The viewer enters the protagonist's mind, seeing what he sees as he sees it. When Terry Malloy drags himself up the gangway and along the dock to the warehouse in *On the Waterfront,* for instance, the camera becomes subjective. As his badly beaten body lurches, the camera jerks around, passing rapidly over faces and then skyward. As he tries to focus his eyes, the camera attempts to focus.

A filmmaker must use strongly subjective devices to show that the camera has become the protagonist. Angles are exaggerated and perspective distorted. As a character tries to remember something, images in the form of **flash frames** (lasting four or five frames) might blip rapidly in and out of his mind, much like the passing memory sensations that occur when a person has a word on the tip of his tongue. Eventually the flashed images might join into a clear, detailed, and coherent memory. Fast and slow motion are also used freely to suggest highly subjective points of view, as are superimposed images and flashbacks. The subjective camera is primarily useful for such exaggerated or distorted states of consciousness as dreams, drug or alcoholic stupors, insanity, or fantasy.

Very few films have been made with an entirely subjective camera. The subjective world in film is too private to be sustained effectively and works best for states in which the mind is consumed by itself. But a mind interested in nothing but itself can hold the interest of others only briefly. Thus insanity is not primarily interesting in and of itself, but rather in its relationship to the world of actualty. The protagonist-as-narrator is a more effective standard for displaying point of view, relying on subjective camera only when appropriate. As with any extreme device, the subjective camera can easily become a gimmick getting in the way of content rather than revealing it. When, on the other hand, subjective camera is used briefly, the results are often startlingly effective.

Subjective camera is the film equivalent of stream-of-consciousness in writing. The subjective camera allows full play to the discrepancy between illusion and reality. The devices of the subjective camera have become conventions: The camera walks by dollying, runs by trucking, twitches or reels by shaking or spinning, becomes dizzy by swish panning (spinning the camera rapidly on its vertical axis), raises or lowers its head by tilting, and so on. Usually, however, shifts to subjective camera are unobtrusive. When a character looks off screen and the next shot shows what he sees, subjective camera has been used in a conventional, barely noticeable, but effective way. Subjective camera is one of the most interesting rhetorical options open to filmmakers because it allows the exploration of the human mind in uniquely cinematic terms.

A filmmaker seldom relies on a single narrative voice. Instead, he switches among the various voices to dramatize his ideas most effectively. The filmmaker's stock-in-trade is the camera-as-narrator, which allows a seemingly passive and objective depiction of reality. To intensify feelings of active involvement or first-hand information, the filmmaker chooses the witness-as-narrator, the protagonist-as-narrator, or the subjective camera.

REALITY SEEN BY THE CAMERA

Film walks a tight line in dealing with point of view because of the discrepancy between the illusion of reality and the reality of illusion. Art is usually less concerned with conveying reality than it is with establishing credibility. Even in episodes that are "true to life" the film artist transcends the simple presentation of actuality to suggest ideas and attitudes toward what is seen. The filmmaker moves beyond "showing" and persuades us to respond in certain ways by manipulating our perceptions.

In life we can find only points of view for complex problems. Truth in human affairs is seldom concrete or simple. Only in entertainment do we expect or accept simple conclusions and simple truths. Life offers no endings with "they lived happily ever after." Indeed, trouble arises when a person tries to apply the logic of "Gunsmoke" to the complex problems of human existence. Yet one might argue that in some cases art can make us aware of the complexities of life, and by doing so make us more capable of handling them. The more a film forces a viewer to come to grips with multiple—and contradictory—points of view, the more capable it makes him of handling the complexity and multiplicity of life.

A story or essay can funnel everything through a single viewpoint. Film cannot because it must normally rely on the tensions among various points of view. Yet it is the dramatic tensions of film that involve a viewer and that ultimately draw him into clashing viewpoints, thrusting upon him the need for response and judgment. The filmmaker exercises his controlling consciousness to select the dominant perspective from which action will be viewed; he decides which elements of a story will be included and which excluded to create a rhetorically effective communication. Part of his voice comes from the way he plays upon subject matter and allows the clashing voices of his characters to reach an audience and to evoke emotional responses. Point of view is partially conveyed by the facts and details marshaled by the filmmaker, but even more important is the emotional milieu in which details are set. The rhetorical devices for creating atmosphere are among the more important tools a filmmaker has to present his view of the world to an audience.

THEME AND UNITY

Pundits often criticize film and television for showing too much violence. Most films and television programs indeed include many and varied violent deaths, acts of brutality, fights, or scenes with one person roughing up another. Saturday and Sunday afternoons find millions perched in front of the tube drinking beer and watching the game. The once attractive rhythm and mood of Saturday at the ballpark are now fodder for middle-aged nostalgia. As television has grown, so have the team-violence-oriented sports such as football and hockey. Did this growth come about by chance? We can have no way of finally knowing what causes the strange and often whimsical tastes of the American people, but something in the visual nature of film and television seems to adapt especially well to clashes between and among people.

CINEMATIC CONFLICT

Conflict or tension energizes almost every work of art, although film probably depends more on scenes of conflict than do most other forms of art. The Taoist emblem of the Yin and Yang perhaps symbolizes best the recurrent struggles of life, and hence of art. Everyone has seen the

Yin and Yang symbol—as the emblem of the old Northern Pacific Railroad if nowhere else. The Yin and Yang symbol represents complementary forces in continuous movement and dynamic struggle. The Yin represents what is passive, dark, moist, cold, negative, and receptive. The Yang suggests the active, light, dry, warm, positive, and penetrating. Each state depends upon the other and neither the Yin nor the Yang can exist alone. Nor can any single state be maintained for long alone, but rather all exist in perpetual and creative change and interaction. The dynamics of conflict propel movement in art much as they motivate men in their daily struggles of ambitions, emotions, ideas, wills, and philosophies.

Conflict in film takes any number of forms. One person might be in conflict with another person (or several different persons), with a group (or with several groups), or with himself. A group (such as a country or a gang) might be in conflict with another group (or several groups). Or an individual (or group) might be in conflict with nature or with the supreme power of a god or gods.

From conflicting forces in a film emerges a series of notions that in turn become central conflicting ideas. Out of the battle of prominent ideas rises the lone dominant or controlling idea, proclaiming its validity to the viewer. From the various images of a film emerges the predominant statement or impression of the **theme**—a controlling idea rendered concrete through the details and progressions of a film.

The theme of a film, as of any artistic work, generates from the controlling consciousness. The voice, discussed in Chapter 4, sets out the tone of the filmmaker's communication with his audience, but it also carries the primary idea that the filmmaker wants to convey. The controlling consciousness and voice must always be considered as something separate from—although related to—the filmmaker. The controlling consciousness centers a film on a single dominant idea; the filmmaker, like any other person, contains within him a great many (often conflicting) ideas. Seldom is one person totally obsessed with a single dominant idea no matter how intense a vision he has to communicate. A theme is a focused idea, made concrete by a set of carefully selected details. Nowhere in life would a concentration of details in relation to an idea be available; this explains in part why many of the same materials can be used to support widely differing ideas. The particular focus and aim of the controlling consciousness define the ways in which details relate to a central theme.

THEME AND THESIS

Like written essays or novels, films depend upon a process of paring a theme from a larger topic. Although one might say a film, novel, or essay is about "cafeterias," no one would venture to communicate simply about "cafeterias." The single word "cafeterias" is not an idea but a topic— and an extremely generalized one at that. Narrowing concern to "cafeterias on college campuses in America" would help by eliminating all other types of cafeterias from consideration. But then the writer or filmmaker must focus even more precisely: Is the history of cafeterias the primary concern? an examination of the quality of food in college cafeterias? The possibilities are endless, and even something such as "facilities necessary in college cafeterias," if handled in full, is too broad for any book or film, much less a student essay.

Once someone begins to get an idea of what he wants to say about a topic, he should be able to phrase his idea briefly. To illustrate the process, we can push on with the topic "cafeterias" by suggesting the rudimentary theme that "cafeterias prepare food poorly." By making a statement about "cafeterias," we have altered the single word "cafeterias" and sent it scurrying in a direction—broad though that direction may still be. Themes are almost always fairly broad ideas defined and sharpened by the filmmaker's materials as a work proceeds. If we add the focus established in the paragraph above about cafeterias on college campuses in America, we can tighten up our theme a bit by saying that "cafeterias on college campuses in America prepare food poorly."

Once we decide to show that "cafeterias on college campuses in America prepare food poorly," we must determine why the food is poorly prepared. From many possibilities we may decide that "cafeterias on college campuses prepare food poorly because they rely on inexperienced and poorly paid help." This statement makes our theme specific enough that it can now be called a thesis. While a theme is a fairly broad idea cementing a work together, a thesis is a rather specific idea, confined in circumstances and requiring some sort of proof. While an essay or a documentary includes a thesis implicitly or explicitly, not all written or film works do. When character rather than idea or theme is central, something as precise as a thesis often cannot be discovered. Rather, works depending upon dramatic development of character frequently do not formulate their ideas in specific enough terms for a thesis.

If we use the above thesis as a starting point for a film, the next step requires selection of details to convey our idea. We may decide to show the preparation of a meal in a typical college cafeteria, considering what is seen to be representative of food preparation in college cafeterias throughout America. Film demands reliance on detail coming from real or potentially real experience because film achieves abstractions mainly by accumulating single details or by juxtaposing images. If we wish to construct a documentary, we will use a real cafeteria and follow the process of food preparation step by step; if we turn to fiction, a carefully plotted story (or satire) will make the same point. All along the line a filmmaker must make choices that will reveal his theme or thesis in the most effective way. Whether a filmmaker develops a theme through character or plot or a thesis through evidence, he must find and use details to make his point.

Through conflicting images and characters the tensions among ideas force a viewer to come to grips with dramatic tensions. Few effective films rely on words to convey ideas and themes. Since film is primarily visual in nature, images bear the burden of communicating. Themes and ideas, which are abstract and elusive by nature, must be spatialized—they must be represented in some physical form operating in physical space. A cook neglecting his frying pork chops while talking with a friend, for instance, will convey "poor food preparation," but a narrator's statement that "cooks sometimes forget to watch closely the food they are cooking" would be less effective in context than visually portraying the cook's actual neglect.

The various tensions a film establishes slowly reveal and reinforce a theme without making simple and obvious what is complex and significant in dramatic context. A theme standing naked and alone sounds both simple and overly familiar. Everyone has repeatedly seen themes lamenting the passing of the "good old days," showing how one determined good man can defeat many men of evil, demonstrating that today's society suffers from "a failure to communicate," or that "war is hell." The list could extend on and on. The theme of a film is seldom unique, but originality of theme seems unimportant to a work of art. The same themes have been used with renewed freshness in work after work for thousands of years.

A theme provides a way of both organizing detail and focusing the concepts a filmmaker seeks to communicate. Hence, a theme clarifies what is always muddled in life because a person cannot easily abstract and separate what is relevant from the seemingly unrelated plethora of events and facts of daily existence. By giving the viewer a handhold, theme helps him grasp what a film is about. For this purpose, the non-originality of a theme becomes valuable, putting the viewer's finger on the map of an area he has visited before. Theme consequently acts as one of the prime tools with which to probe, criticize, study, or to analyze what a film is about.

Most films are both instruments of communication and works of art. Rhetorical methods seldom exist apart from esthetic considerations. If an audience cannot comprehend or be moved by a film, the work fails both rhetorically and esthetically. Since theme is the chief point of focus for all esthetic and rhetorical considerations, a filmmaker's first thoughts are usually toward the clarification of theme. Without such clarification, elaborate camera angles, sophisticated acting, or imaginative sets will all be wasted. Imbedded in a film's theme is the total significance of a filmmaker's efforts and a work's intent.

A thesis may be one type of theme, but a theme certainly need not be a thesis. A great many films offer no message at all even though controlled by a theme and by an ever-present operative point of view. Consider, for example, any of the short films made in recent years showing abstract patterns of light and color moving in synchronization with music. Carefree tempos or balletlike rhythms become themes, ordering and organizing a film. Even commercial films, such as *A Man and a Woman* or *Elvira Madigan,* concern themselves more with a thematic mood than a thematic message. A viewer recalls such films more in terms of moods than ideas.

Although themes can grow out of almost any unifying principle, most films rely on themes projecting a "point." Themes trying to make a statement grow from a variety of concerns: emotional, psychological, ethical, political, religious, social, and philosophical, to name a few. Frequently themes generate from a filmmaker's concept of how men should relate to their societies or how their societies should respond to them. To say a filmmaker sets out to prove his point as a lawyer sets out to prove his case would vastly oversimplify the rhetorical process. Most filmmakers do not try to prove something as clear-cut as innocence or guilt. Thematic points frequently bounce against other ideas, creating a dynamic tension allowing the implications and complications of a message to be considered and revealed. At his best, a filmmaker highlights the nuances of problems rather than offering easy solutions. The "point" is a way of focusing attention and of controlling and explaining the significance of the flow of images. What happens beyond and outside of the "point" is often of greatest significance.

GOOD THEMES AND BAD MOVIES

Stacking good films against bad helps show why the isolated theme is not of prime significance, although its effectiveness as a controlling principle is. Any night's viewing of standard television fare will furnish an adequate supply of bad films. An array of themes, as well as devices, will be exploited to shock, amaze, and titillate the viewer while preventing a hand from reaching toward that too-easily-turned dial. Indeed, the dial probably will not be turned even though the watcher knows he is consenting to watch junk. The bad western will once again shock as the viewer witnesses justice, truth, and beauty triumph as blood stains the floor of the saloon for the fifty-second straight week. The outnumbered good-guy marshal must overcome evil again and again. Although the viewer can become engrossed, not much of complexity happens in such shows, and the viewer gains few insights since he has seen identical themes, plots, and characters many times before. The possible ways of presenting any theme—effectively or poorly—are infinite, although the poor ways seem as recurrent as the men who "need killing" in the westerns.

A theme in itself will give a viewer no guide to movie quality, but a bad film's lack of integration will. The theme of a good film is a springboard—but not for the usual clichés. Few statements could sound more trite than the badly stated themes of most good films. But effectiveness occurs in the handling of a theme and in the application of fresh material to the recurrent problems of life. The bad film isolates theme from detail, offering abstract statement and carved-up sets of episodes with all the standard lines used before and without bothering to insert images with their own energy. The conflict between a marshal and outlaw or between any other combination of people can have no force if a filmmaker has not bothered to create tensions with depth. A bad man who is bad because he wears black, slaps a girl, and robs a stagecoach cannot dynamically interact with a marshal who is simply there to preserve law and order.

The question of the evils of hackneyed entertainment films is, it would seem, personal. But is it? Are there social consequences to trite films? Cliché and pandering to the public taste always seem to live under a common-law marriage. Films catering to popular desires knowingly manipulate emotions (and therefore social attitudes) through the ready-made "phrases" of film. Those who know the right rhetorical tricks can arouse sympathy, hostility, affection, and other feelings with remarkable ease. The beautiful girl struggling to regain the use of her legs always brings tears. The orphan, seen from a high angle as he stands alone and afraid in a hostile world, evokes strong sympathies. The braggart, with face leering in close-up, continues to arouse hostility.

Yet, it must be admitted that no one really knows what the final results of media manipulation are. And who can distinguish in entertainment films between what might be harmful in manipulation and what provides people with the particular fantasies or fictional experiences needed to make life coherent or bearable?

As a mass art, film reflects the interests and concerns of a period. The white-telephone films of the 1930s (so-called because of the sumptuous settings in houses replete with white telephones, symbols of conspicuous wealth) revealed the hopes of depression-struck America. The natures of heroes also shed light on a time and on people's aspirations. As a colleague once remarked when we were showing *Casablanca* for a class, "Students can't understand Humphrey Bogart without understanding their parents a little bit better." It is always easiest to see viewer expectations in films of the past and to spot crass audience manipulation for what it is when we no longer care about the reasons for it. The difficulty comes in distinguishing the *ways* contemporary filmmakers play upon the expectations of their audiences. Confronting contemporary manipulation brings us face to face with ourselves.

A critical viewer's primary concern must be with the way a filmmaker handles his theme, not with the way a theme agrees with or contradicts native sensibilities. The point can and should be identified, but not simplified. A film trying only to entertain quickly identifies itself. The viewer need not struggle to grasp the theme nor work to understand any nuances. Simple enjoyment is enough. (And everyone knows the world needs more of that!) But pablum makes for a bland diet. Art, on the other hand, moves beyond entertainment, challenging and making demands on a viewer.

Fueled with powerful images, the viewer of a first-rate film can leave the comforting turnpike provided by the theme and investigate the temptations of the side roads, always able to return and maintain bearings via the theme. Even after a film has ended, the process continues. Sometimes the images of a film will recur for days (sometimes years) in the imagination, asking for reinvestigation and reapplication. The recurrence of such images cannot be explained simply in terms of the theme binding them together, and the mysteries and ambiguities causing the mind continually to play over them can never be fully explained. But the magic can in part be explained by the union of idea and image made in probing a fundamental concern of the human psyche.

In developing a theme, a filmmaker constantly faces a dilemma—should he disguise his point or transcend it? The first assumes an intent to communicate a rather specific idea. For example, if a filmmaker wants to adopt the theme that "any society is damaged by participating in war" his tendency might be to show as emphatically as possible that an immoral war in Vietnam has needlessly torn apart the fabric of our society. A big order, to say the least. He might show streams of images of individual destruction caused by the war, probably juxtaposed (ironically in many cases) to what has happened in various segments of our society, from corporations to the ghettoes, as the war has continued. In other words, the filmmaker would rally every effective image coming from real events to support his point—a point narrow in scope and applicable primarily to a relatively brief period in history. But those images would require careful control and the right dressing unless the filmmaker assumes an audience fully agreeing with him. If he intends to persuade, though, he must assume that his audience has no opinion, is indifferent to the problem, or has a contrary opinion. In any case, he will manipulate his images in such a way that his point will be disguised. In the clothing of objective documentary or of some other form, the message of the filmmaker will be made acceptable to the intended audience. The film-maker's goal would be immediate and clear, and he would arrange all evidence for no other purpose than to persuade his audience to his view-point on the war.

On the other hand, the filmmaker could opt to handle his point in a less transitory way, primarily by not anchoring his film to a specific set of historically identifiable events. His method in the first case would probably be documentary; in the second case, fictional. If he wished to transcend his theme, his intents would be less specifically propagandistic than in the first case. Rather than aiming for the gut, he would aim for the quick of the human spirit. Rather than concentrating on a single war, his theme would probably suggest something about all war, center-ing on the recurrent nature of human actions.

Whether a film is transitory or goes deeper depends on the way the filmmaker treats his materials. Most people have seen documentary footage of the horrors of the Nazi concentration camps, and there can be no doubt that this footage condemns those responsible for the evils of the camps. But those who have seen Alain Resnais' *Night and Fog* have seen documentary footage handled in a much more potent and significant way than that found in any ordinary documentation of events. In the hands of this master film artist, footage of the concentration camps becomes not as much a condemnation of the Nazis as it is a statement reminding the viewer that the Nazis were not an anomaly of history. Resnais blends his factual materials into an extraordinarily powerful statement about the potential bestiality of all mankind. By not opting for simple persuasion about the wrongs of a particular set of historical events, Resnais transcends his theme, asserting what is human rather than what is doctrinal. A film such as *Night and Fog* demonstrates that an artist can effectively straddle (or conjoin) the worlds of propaganda and art.

The way a theme combines with its images is too magical to dissect logically in a well-wrought film. A weak film makes the relationship between theme and image too tentative and too obvious. The filmmaker who tries to impose his ideas on the world by selectively illustrating what he says may have temporary successes, but ultimately his work will fail. The magic fusing of theme to image demands focus on human images and human truths. And once the filmmaker seeks to transcend rather than merely illustrate his theme, he faces the task of gathering images unsullied by the taint of cliché.

Since a filmmaker does not announce his intentions, a viewer must tilt with a film on his own. He must look for small signs revealing a film's purpose. Everyone has a threshold at which he realizes a film simply seeks to propagandize or titillate. (Propaganda and titillation are mutual variants of the same process: Propaganda exploits emotion for a particular end; titillation exploits emotion for the profit of those showing the film.) Generally, a viewer's awareness that a filmmaker is exploiting emotion comes through recognition of an apparent discrepancy between theme or thesis and supporting images. Frequently images simply are not strong enough to sustain a theme. For example, scenes of German (or American) concentration camps will not support the idea that Germans (or Americans) are brutal people. The scenes may shock, but the theme soon collapses, often leaving viewers startled and possibly indignant, but unenlightened. A viewer must question the emotions a film's images produce and decide whether they work together well enough to support the idea a filmmaker suggests by direct or indirect statement.

SCRIPT

The process of interweaving theme and images begins, surprisingly, with the written word. The script is generally the blueprint of a film. Since only the celluloid image reaches a viewer's eyes, he easily overlooks the significance of the script. Unlike the scripts of dramas, film scripts receive scant attention. Primarily only film buffs read scripts. (At the same time the number of persons reading scripts is on the increase, if the recent surge in publication of paperback scripts is a fair indicator.)

The fact that few people read film scripts signals the rightful dominance of the medium of film. Script reading cannot substitute for film viewing. At best, reading a script lets the reader slowly reconstruct in his mind a film he has already seen. The process allows the mind to arrest the forward motion of a film and to consider and savor the development at a speed the reader chooses. Yet the script experience cannot substitute for the pleasures of the film experience—as happens in drama.

When compared with dramatic scripts, film scripts seem little concerned with dialogue, focusing chiefly on visual images. The primary rhetorical thrust of drama, on the other hand, comes from verbal language; this language can be recorded on the printed page and the reader can construct in his imagination the sparse sets used in most drama. A drama has no permanent form, but a reader, a director, or an actor reconstructs and alters a work every time it is read or peformed. Films, on the other hand, rely most heavily on visual rhetoric. A playgoer listens first and watches second; a film viewer watches first and listens second. In film, verbal rhetoric takes a back seat to visual rhetoric.

Because of film's emphasis on visuals, the verbal language recorded in a script tells little of the ultimate impact of a film. As a blueprint, a script provides patterns of structure, unity, coherence, and sound and image symbols, but it provides little to help the reader construct or reconstruct a film. Rather, it helps the director to create the most appropriate visual images since it constantly points out the ways a theme must be developed.

A dramatic script is finished once the writer yanks it from his typewriter for the last time. The same act is often only a middle stage in the life of a film script. From the original writer it may be passed on to other writers as part of an assembly line. Once it leaves the hands of the writers it is occasionally reworked in written form by others along the line (such as the producer or the company censor), then it is altered in the process of filming and compiling by the director, by the cameraman, and by the editor. Each of these people has a say in what the final product will be. No other artistic form involves so many changes at so many levels of production.

Because the visual image is of primary concern, film is a director's medium. Necessary as a blueprint is, the film image is of ultimate importance. Yet the quality of that image frequently depends on the quality of the script. David Lean, one of the best-known contemporary directors, considers a script the most important aspect of a film and declares that a good film cannot be made out a bad script. Because the script is the blueprint of a film, a bad blueprint will make a bad film. The fact that viewers seldom see the blueprint (as the blueprint of a house is seldom looked at by those who live in it) does not alter its importance. The script articulates the ideas a film will explore and establishes the line of development and rhythms a director will follow.

The relationship of film to script varies so much that generalizations are difficult. Some directors and writers collaborate and a film's final version closely parallels the writer's conception. (The collaboration between Alain Resnais and Alain Robbe-Grillet on *Last Year at*

Marienbad offers a notable example.) In other cases a writer and director may have entirely different conceptions of what a film should be, and the pages of Hollywood's history are full of writers calling "foul" to the way directors have treated their scripts. Sometimes directors, such as Bergman and Antonioni, write their own scripts, marrying conception and realization.

Scripts also vary in detail. Some provide only a skeletal framework and the filmmaker works largely by improvising; others provide for almost every detail of movement and scene, advising on such matters as dialogue cadence, delivery of key lines, and editing instructions. In any case, a writer provides a director with a foundation upon which a pleasing and effective superstructure can be built. As an example of a detailed script in which writer and director are in almost perfect accord, consider the opening pages of the script for *Last Year at Marienbad,* written by Alain Robbe-Grillet and directed by Alain Resnais:

> Opening with a romantic, passionate, violent burst of music, the kind used at the end of films with powerfully emotional climaxes (a large orchestra of strings, woodwinds, brasses, etc.), the credits are initially of a classical type: the names in fairly simple letters, black against a gray background, or white against a gray background; the names or groups of names are framed with simple lines. These frames follow each other at a normal, even rather slow, rhythm.
>
> Then the frames are gradually transformed, grow broader, are embellished with various curlicues which finally constitute a kind of picture frame, at first flat, then painted in *trompe-l'oeil* so as to appear to be three dimensional.
>
> Finally, in the last credits, the frames are real, complex and covered with ornaments. At the same time, the margin around them has widened slightly, revealing a little of the wall where these pictures are hung, the wall itself decorated with gilded moldings and carved woodwork.
>
> The last two credit titles, instead of constituting separate shots, are gradually revealed by a lateral movement of the camera which, without stopping on the first frame when it is centered, continues its slow, regular movement, passes across a section of the wall containing only woodwork, gilding, molding, etc., then reaches the last frame, containing the last name or names of the credits, which could begin by less important names and end with the major ones, or even mix them, especially toward the end. This last picture has a considerable margin of wall around it, as if it were seen from farther away. The camera passes across this without stopping, then continues its movement along the wall.
>
> Parallel to the development of the image during the credits, the music has gradually been transformed into a man's voice—slow, warm, fairly loud but with a certain neutral quality at the same time: a fine theatrical voice, rhythmical but without any particular emotion.
>
> This voice speaks continuously, but although the music has stopped completely, we cannot yet understand the words (or in any case we under-

stand them only with the greatest difficulty) because of a strong reverberation or some effect of the same sort (two identical sound tracks staggered, gradually superimposing until the voice becomes a normal one).

X's voice: *Once again—[1] I walk on, once again, down these corridors, through these halls, these galleries, in this structure—of another century; this enormous, luxurious, baroque, lugubrious hotel—where corridors succeed endless corridors—silent deserted corridors overloaded with a dim, cold ornamentation of woodwork, stucco, moldings, marble, black mirrors, dark paintings, columns, heavy hangings—sculptured door frames, series of doorways, galleries—transverse corridors that open in turn on empty salons, rooms overloaded with an ornamentation from another century, silent halls. . . .*

Beginning at the end of the credits, the camera continues its slow, straight, uniform movement down a sort of gallery of which only one side is seen, fairly dark, lit only by regularly spaced windows on the other side. There is no sunshine, it may even be twilight. But the electric lights are not on; at regular intervals, a lighter area, opposite each invisible window, shows more distinctly the moldings that cover the wall.

The field of the image includes the entire wall, from top to bottom, with a thin strip of the floor or the ceiling, or both. The shot is not taken from directly opposite the wall, but at a slight angle (toward the direction in which the camera advances).[2]

Alain Robbe-Grillet's script, however, is not typical of film scripts—a circumstance that should not be surprising since he is primarily a novelist. Robbe-Grillet describes scenes in detail as he wishes them to appear, but he does not use the normal terminology and format of a film script. Following are the beginnings to four scripts providing a sense of the form in which film scripts typically appear. Note especially the numbering of shots, the time in seconds given to the reader, and the way shots are usually set up to contain dialogue and action.

Henry V[3]

L.S. *Aerial View of London in 1600.* CAMERA TRACKS BACK *to reveal the City in extreme* L.S. *then* TRACKS *in to centre first the Bear Playhouse and then the Globe Playhouse. A flag is being hoisted up the Standard of this Playhouse.*

C.S. *The Globe Playhouse Flag unfurling and fluttering.*

---

[1] The dash represents a slight pause, more emphatic than the meaning of the text suggests.

[2] Alain Robbe-Grillet, *Last Year at Marienbad*, trans. Richard Howard (New York: Grove Press, 1962), pp. 17–19.

[3] Laurence Olivier and Reginald Beck, "Henry V," *Film Scripts One*, ed. George P. Garrett, O. B. Hardison, Jr., and Jane R. Gelfman (New York: Appleton-Century-Crofts, 1971), pp. 41–42.

MUSIC STOPS.

M.C.S.   *Main in Globe Playhouse on small platform at foot of flagpole. He tightens the flag rope and makes it secure. He blows two fanfares.* CAMERA TRACKS DOWN TO *Orchestra Gallery below him.*

ORCHESTRA STARTS TO PLAY.

CAMERA PANS LEFT *to show people filling the top gallery of theatre.* CAMERA *continues panning round and down to the second gallery. A girl drops a handkerchief out of picture.*

M.L.S. THE THIRD GALLERY.   *A man catches the handkerchief.* CAMERA PANS LEFT *to the ground floor entrance where the people are coming in. An Orange Seller steps down into the theatre.*

M.S.   *The Orange Girl walking into the Theatre offering her wares,* CAMERA PANS LEFT *with her and* TRACKS SLOWLY BACK *to reveal the auditorium in L.S. with the stage in background. A prompter gives a signal to the Orchestra to play a fanfare.*

MUSIC STOPS.

M.L.S.   *Low angle shot the Orchestra Gallery. Man blows a* FANFARE.

L.S. AUDITORIUM WITH STAGE IN B.G.   *A boy comes through the curtains on to the stage and holds a board up to the audience.*

M.C.S. SIDE ANGLE OF THE BOY.   *He swings the board to camera on which is written—*

> The Chronicle History of
> HENRY THE FIFTH
> *with his battle fought at Agin Court.*

L. HIGH ANGLE SHOT FROM THE TOP GALLERY.   *Audience in f.g. The boy on the stage swings the board and exits through the curtains. Chorus enters and bows. Audience applauds.*

Rashomon by Akira Kurosawa[4]

The title sequence consists of some ten shots of the half-ruined gate, Rashomon, in the rain. Superimposed over these are the title and credits, including, in the prints distributed in the United States, vignettes (oval-shaped insets) showing the major characters in action. Various details of the gate are seen, its steps, the base of a column, the eaves of the roof,

---

[4] Akira Kurosawa and Shinobu Hashimoto, *Rashomon,* ed. Donald Richie (New York: Grove Press, 1969), pp. 11–15.

puddles on the ground. Everywhere there is evidence of the downpour. Gagaku, traditional court music, is heard during the credits, then the sound of the torrential rain.

The final title reads: "Kyoto, in the twelfth century, when famines and civil wars had devastated the ancient capital."

1   LONG SHOT. Two men, a priest and a woodcutter, are sitting motionless, taking shelter under the gate. (4 seconds)

2   MEDIUM SHOT from the side of the two, the woodcutter in the foreground, as they stare out at the rain with heads bowed. The woodcutter raises his head.

Woodcutter: I can't understand it. I just can't understand it at all. (16)

3   CLOSE-UP of the priest; he looks at the woodcutter and back again at the rain. (11)

4   LS from directly in front. The two men continue to stare vacantly at the rain. (5)

5   A GENERAL VIEW of the gate; a man enters from behind the camera and runs toward the gate; splashing through puddles. Thunder is heard. (15)

6   LS from reverse angle. The man runs past a fallen column, and disappears from the frame. (2)

7   MS of the steps of the gate; he enters from behind the camera and runs up the steps to shelter. (4)

8   MS. Out of the rain, he turns and looks back outside, then removes a rag covering his head and wrings it out. The woodcutter's voice is heard off-camera.

Woodcutter *(off):*   I just can't understand it. (11)

9   LS. The newcomer, in the background, turns toward the priest and woodcutter, who are sitting in the foreground. (3)

10   MS of the newcomer. He goes toward the others—the camera panning with him—and sits down behind the woodcutter.

Commoner: What's the matter? (25)

11   MS of the woodcutter and commoner.

Commoner: What can't you understand?

Woodcutter: I've never heard of anything so strange.

Commoner: Why don't you tell me about it? (13)

The 400 Blows by François Truffaut[5]

TITLE SEQUENCE. *The title sequence consists of a number of traveling shots of the Eiffel Tower, taken from different angles and streets; a variety of Parisian architecture appears in the foreground. The theme music continues throughout the sequence. (158 seconds)*

1 CLOSE-UP *of a schoolroom desk, seen from over the shoulder of a young boy. He is writing. He puts down his pen and pulls a pin-up picture of a girl in a bathing suit out of the desk.*

After a quick look he passes it ahead and the picture moves rapidly up one row and across three. As the camera pans we see the class: a group of perhaps forty boys, twelve or thirteen years old, anxiously keeping up the appearance of studying for their teacher, who sits at a large desk in front. (He is known to the students as "Little Quiz.") The pin-up makes its way to Antoine Doinel, a dark-haired boy in a turtleneck sweater. He draws a moustache on the picture.

Little Quiz: Doinel! Bring me what you have there.

Antoine reluctantly walks up to the teacher, a dour-looking man in a full-length coat, and hands him the picture.

Little Quiz: Ah! Very nice! Go stand in the corner!

Antoine goes to the corner and disappears behind a small blackboard which stands on an easel. He reappears momentarily on the other side of the easel holding his nose and grimacing. The class laughs.

Little Quiz: Quiet! Only a minute left!

Class: Oh!

Little Quiz: Quiet!

He moves between the rows of students. (56)

2 MEDIUM SHOT. *The teacher walks to the back of the classroom. The students are bent over their papers in deep concentration—except for René Bigey, who stares at the ceiling looking for inspiration.*

Little Quiz: The papers will be collected in thirty seconds.

Protests from the class.

Little Quiz: Quiet!

He walks to the front of the room, stopping to encourage a tousle-headed boy by cuffing him on the head.

Little Quiz: *(looking at his watch):*   Monitors get ready. I'll count three. One . . . two . . . three . . . Collect the papers!

---

[5] François Truffaut and Marcel Moussy, *The 400 Blows*, ed. David Denby (New York: Grove Press, 1969), pp. 11–14.

Student monitors spring to their feet. René gets a sudden inspiration and begins writing; the others lift their heads and slap down their pens. (34)

3 MEDIUM CLOSE-UP. René is writing furiously. Bertrand Mauricet tries to collect his paper, but René pushes him away.

René: Collect the papers in the back!

Little Quiz: *(off)*: What's going on?

Mauricet: He won't give me his paper, sir.

Little Quiz: *(off)*: No favoritism.

Mauricet finally pulls the paper away.

René *(to Mauricet)*: Brown-nose! (16)

Ivan the Terrible by Sergei Eisenstein[6]

PART I

Shot 1. The credits unfold against a background of black clouds driven before an approaching storm whilst a CHOIR sings, off.

CHOIR *off:*   'A black cloud is forming
          A bloody dawn approaching.
          The boyars have hatched a treacherous plot
          Against the Tsar's authority
          Which they are now unleashing.'

At the end of the credits the following title flashes across the screen:

TITLE: This film tells the story of the man who was the first to unite our country four hundred years ago: the Archduke of Moscow who welded greedy, warring and divided principalities into a single, powerful State . . . a military leader who made the glory of Russian arms resound in the East as in the West . . . a sovereign who resolved his country's cruel dilemmas by having himself crowned the first Tsar of all the Russias.

Shot 2. The sound of the CHOIR fades out. Interior of the Dormition Cathedral. High angle medium close-up of the Monomakh crown as all the Cathedral bells ring out. This sound continues throughout most of the scene.

Shot 3. MEDIUM CLOSE-UP of the TSAR's regalia: the sceptre and orb.

Shot 4. Long-shot of the cathedral: the coronation is in progress. PIMEN, Metropolitan Archbishop of Moscow, enters through the monumental

---

[6] Sergei Eisenstein, *Ivan the Terrible*, ed. Sandra Wake (New York: Simon and Schuster, 1970), pp. 25–26.

Holy Door. Like those attending on him he wears full ceremonial robes. He halts and raises his arms to bless the congregation as he advances towards camera.

Shot 5. CLOSE-UP *of him.*

Pimen: In the name of . . .

Shot 6. LONG-SHOT *of the congregation in the cathedral, which bows and crosses itself.*

Pimen: *continues off:*   . . . the Father, the Son and the Holy Ghost . . .

Shot 7. LONG-SHOT, *slightly high angle, of the congregation standing, seen between the columns of the Sanctuary.*

Pimen: *continues off:*   . . . the Archduke and Sovereign Ivan Vassilie-vich . . .

Shot 8. MEDIUM CLOSE-UP *of* PIMEN.

Pimen *continues:*   . . . is crowned Tsar of Moscow.

Shot 9.   A group of FOREIGN AMBASSADORS *are seen in long-shot, wearing impressive white ruffs. They follow the ceremony from a corner of the cathedral.*

Shot 10.   Shot of a member of the congregation gazing at the scene through square-lensed spectacles.

Pimen *continues off:*   . . . anointed of God . . .

Shot 11. LONG-SHOT, *slightly high angle, of the listening congregation.*

UNITY

A script serves primarily to provide a focus for artistic control. It establishes a sense of direction and indicates what materials will be put together to carry out a film's theme. **Unity** occurs at that point where filmmaker applies detail to theme. In preparing a script, and even in actual shooting, a writer and director constantly choose which details will be included and which excluded. The film we earlier proposed to make about the poor quality of cafeteria food would require concentrating on images carrying out our central idea. Seldom would we wish to show a student waking up, rubbing his eyes, lying still another five minutes, getting up, washing, shaving, dressing, and undertaking all the other necessities of the first hour of the morning. These details would be irrelevant in most cases. We do not need to see a student wash his face; the detail does nothing to extend the meaning of our theme about the poor quality of cafeteria food. Irrelevant scenes would collapse any sense of unity, confusing a viewer.

Art allows very few irrelevancies. When we see the camera play up an action or gesture, we expect the gesture or detail to contain meaning. Life itself is a hodge-podge; unrelated things happen simultaneously. But for reasons too complex to examine here, we expect an artist to focus on the theme he establishes for his work. Each shot must be included for a reason. The controlling consciousness must be sure that each detail aligns with a thematic principle. In a sense, the care with which a film-maker adapts detail to theme and carefully assembles one well-chosen detail after another in an effectively planned order is at the core of what is good art. Bad art seems to rely on what happens to be convenient; the filmmaker thinks little about the applicability of details if they seem right at first glance. But a first-rate filmmaker's mind always seems to have played upon details ahead of our minds; as a viewer probes details and considers them, he senses that a filmmaker has thought about why and how particular details are used. His controlling consciousness has pervaded all aspects of his work, considering each image in terms of his central theme.

Unity involves the creative linking of our emotional and intellectual powers. Consider the ways unity appears in life. The people of a unified country agree generally with the goals and directions of their country and work for them with a single spirit. The unity of marriage suggests that two partners with separate identities merge into a single unit larger than its parts. Unity implies the agreement of all parts, with each segment contributing to the purpose and direction of the whole.

Unity works on many levels in film. Once a filmmaker establishes a dominant movement, either in terms of shots or theme, he must sustain it. For example, if a film treats the westward migration, showing the usual movement of wagons and people from right to left, the filmmaker must be careful to avoid taking any shot from the opposite side of the wagons. By suddenly showing left-to-right movement of the same people on wagons, the unity of right-to-left rhythms would be broken. All matters of filmmaking, from sound to acting, must be coordinated behind the theme to achieve unity.

STRUCTURE
AND ORGANIZATION

Although a theme provides a foundation for a film, a foundation has little value standing alone. The foundation of a film, like that of a house, exists in order to have a structure built on it. Ultimately it is the structure of a work, and its adornments, that attracts the eye and challenges the mind. Of course, not all aspects of structure are easily observable, but they are still at work providing a framework and organizing a film's elements into coherent patterns. Even though a viewer may not consciously recognize a film's structural patterns, they nevertheless lead him from shot to shot, scene to scene, and sequence to sequence. Without structure, both unity and coherence would remain impossibilities, since the structure of a film determines what is necessary and what is irrelevant in developing a cinematic theme.

OPENINGS

Unlike the dramatist, the filmmaker is able to initiate action rapidly and to move elliptically through a chain of events. A filmmaker normally selects details that quickly clarify his theme, spending little time on exposition not immediately relevant. (Exposition establishes setting,

112

introduces characters, and provides background information.) The opening, or exposition, of a film typically flows more directly into the mainstream of a work's events than does the beginning of a play. The opening of a film usually establishes its foundation by delineating a theme, consequently suggesting (without telling all) the directions that plot and character will take. Usually subordinate themes or motifs appear in preparation for their later development.

Films focus less than most dramas on conveying information at the opening and more on setting up a mood with such emotional force that a viewer will be prepared to share the experiences and feelings of other characters. Concentrating on involvement rather than information, film draws in a viewer immediately and provides necessary information later as a narrative progresses. An opening thus has more significance as an emotional premise than as a logical or intellectual one. After an initial thematic and emotional pattern is well established, a film can go on to explore relationships and fresh variations of theme. The opening peek a viewer has of a theme progresses (or should do so) to a larger vision by a film's end.

If, for example, we were to make the film on the poor quality of food served in college cafeterias suggested in the preceding chapter, we would probably not begin with the hiring of cooks, even though some aspects of that might be important (and later included). Rather, we would seek images setting up the theme of "the poor quality of food served in college cafeterias" and use these for the introduction. The initial point might be made effectively by showing an indifferent cook preparing mashed potatoes by dumping in salt and milk without any regard to quantity and then only slightly whipping the lumpy potatoes before serving them. As our narrative developed, we might then add relevant bits about the hiring of cooks, but the emotional tone would already be firmly established.

CONFLICT

In setting up the emotional climate of an opening, a filmmaker also spells out the central conflicts emerging from the narrative line. From the beginning, a viewer consciously or unconsciously starts choosing sides. The choices vary: marshal or outlaw, hunter or hunted, man or nature, cops or robbers, Israeli army or Arab army. The **protagonist**, who is the focus of attention, generates the action. Pitted against him is the **antagonist**, who tries to thwart the intents of the protagonist. The protagonist or antagonist need not be people; forces such as nature, animals, or society can fill either role. Whenever conflict is present—and it must be present either by implication or by active participation—protagonist and antagonist can be identified. Each takes his identity from his relationship to the theme.

The generating action of a film depends on the internal struggle of the protagonist as he moves toward one of two antithetical possibilities: good or evil, life or death, kindness or cruelty, love or hate, freedom or chains. Whatever choice he makes, the antagonist will attempt to thwart him and prevent him from reaching his goal. If the protagonist is headed toward a life of crime, the antagonist might try to stop him or even to turn him to a life of good. The protagonist makes choices and generates action, but this role does not determine whether he is "good" or "bad." He can be hero or villain, but he must be the center of attention and make the first choice determining the direction and nature of the central conflict of a film. The conventional pattern, though, is for the protagonist to be a "hero" who moves toward "good" while the antagonist satanically tries to lead the hero toward evil deeds.

Unlike the beginnings of novel or drama, the first five minutes of cinema are crucial in their development of conflict. Not only is the viewer drawn in, but he is prepared emotionally for what will follow. Television shows frequently put almost everything they have into the first five minutes to draw and keep viewers. There are, of course, serious drawbacks to producing maximum intensity in the first five minutes of a television show. Everything else goes downhill since the show promises much more than can possibly be delivered. Usually television achieves initial intensity by depicting extremes of violence or climaxes of interpersonal struggles. As an alternative to starting at the highest point, many television programs now present significant and action-filled excerpts from the middle of a show as a way of drawing in the audience; once this is achieved (and after an advertisement) normal progression of events begins.

Films need not go to the extremes of television. The audience for a film cannot switch channels, nor are people likely to walk out after five minutes when they have paid to see a film. Freedom from the fickleness of the television audience allows a filmmaker a more artistic use of the first five minutes. He has a clear opportunity to set a viable emotional tone and to promise thematic developments that he can indeed fulfill.

From the opening on, a filmmaker structures his work on the thematic relationship between conflicting forces of characters. Unlike the theater, which usually depicts a mounting series of crises culminating in a final gargantuan crisis, film builds cumulative experiences to a point of maximum intensity. Cinematic conflict generally develops fluidly, mounting inexorably to a point of climax. Rather than building up pressure and then releasing the audience for a while with minor climaxes, film tends to maintain increasing pressure with each development, offering an audience few "breathers." Lacking the long breaks after scene and act available to drama, film must maintain pressure, tightening the screw with each turn of the action.

LITERARY PATTERNS

The most basic patterns of organization generally applied to dramas, however, fit film equally as well. Films almost always have clear beginnings, middles, and ends. The beginning introduces a character in a situation, with the differences in emphasis and action noted earlier. The middle reveals characters or forces in conflict, leading to a point where a character changes his situation or is changed by it. The ending resolves the central conflict, bringing the film to a close.

In the mid-nineteenth century, Gustav Freytag proposed what has become in some circles a byword of dramatic structure. Freytag's system plots the action of a play like a pyramid on a graph. An **introduction** establishes tone, setting, characters, and necessary facts. **Rising action** (also called **complication**) is set in motion by an initial choice by the protagonist and moves through elevating stages of conflict to the **climax,** or turning point. The **falling action** begins at this point, stressing the actions of forces opposing the hero and maintaining a degree of suspense. The **denouement** involves the death of the tragic hero and wraps up all the loose ends.

It would be convenient if Freytag's schema applied to dramas, much less to films. It works very neatly with some classical tragedies, but only by pounding round pegs into square holes will it fit many dramas and most films. Even if the apparent proportion of each section is ignored, the system still will not work. If dramatists or filmmakers intentionally worked with Freytag's schema in mind, it would indeed work. But they do not and it does not. (In fairness, though, one must add that Freytag's triangle can be modified into a patchwork of superimposed triangles as a useful method of diagraming structurally. Each kind of conflict can be given its own triangle, thus providing some insight into the interrelationships of conflict.)

Yet shaping and organizing do take place on a higher plane than beginning, middle, and end. There simply is no standard formula for organization, but rather a large number of structures erected to fit the needs of various films. House-builders can rely on prefabricated structures, but filmmakers cannot. Each story line presents unique problems of structure, although a story also contains its own organizational seeds. A journey, for example, provides an opportunity for a series of loosely related episodes, each with its own beginning, climax, and end.

The organizing principles open to a filmmaker resemble those available to the dramatist, or (most important of all) the novelist or essayist. It is the wide range of options open to a filmmaker that makes meaningless Freytag's narrow structural pattern based on five-act dramas. Depending on whether he wishes to work with fiction or documentary, a filmmaker can select from the wealth of organizing principles available to any writer: linear or cyclical (following straight chronology or returning to the place or time of origin); static or progressive; inductive (from particulars to general statements) or deductive (from general statements to particulars), and so on.

Although some writers, especially of novels, rely on time as an organizing principle, most choose logically conceived structures. **Chronology,** however, is the most common broad organizing principle used by filmmakers. A film might depict a single day in the life of a person, the cyclical process of a year (beginning, say, with spring and birth, moving through summer and maturity, fall and middle age, winter and approaching death, and finally touching briefly again on spring and the process of rebirth), or the life span of a man (Richard Nixon's humble Quaker beginnings, school, college, law practice, the Senate, vice-president, defeat for President, defeat for governor of California, back to law, then President, old age, and death). Simple chronology adapts best to documentary and its fictional cousins because it provides an environment for the step-by-step revelation of actual events. Even cyclical time appears mostly in documentaries since an emphasis on cycles usually centers on some aspect of nature.

CAUSE AND EFFECT

Cause and effect is an organizational method that is particularly useful at the level of scene but also structures entire films on occasion. Film adapts especially well to this method since a viewer assumes that the first thing he sees in time actually occurs first. Shot two is always affected by and read in terms of shot one. An experiment by Leo Kuleshov, the early Russian film theorist and teacher, makes the point. He first filmed a close-up of an actor with an expressionless face. Then Kuleshov juxtaposed the face to three other shots in the following order: a bowl of soup on a table, expressionless face; a dead woman in a casket, expressionless face; a child playing with a toy bear, expressionless face. The audience did not realize that Kuleshov used the same actor's face each time. The result? Raves for the skill of the actor in each instance! The viewers thought that he showed a heavy pensive mood over forgotten soup, deep sorrow for the dead woman, and a happy look while watching the child at play. Each shot *caused* the audience to read the next shot in a certain way. *Set* is the word modern psychologists use for this process; a set is a readiness to respond in a certain way. A set can come from preconceptions or prejudices, or it can result in film from one shot preceding and thus preparing the way for another. The same process continues throughout a film. A viewer reads information in terms of what he has seen already. Cause and effect works on both the high and low levels of structure. By rhetorically manipulating his materials, a filmmaker establishes the "truth" of what causes what. Selection and ordering of material can, for example, make either police or demonstrators seem to cause a riot. By the right ordering of images, the cause of a man's robbing a store may appear to be society, family pressures, or the man's own immortality. Once initial causes become established, a cause-effect sequence often begins. For instance, the bad guy robs the bank; the marshal chases him; the marshal shoots the bad guy's brother; seeking revenge, the bad guy hunts the marshal, and so on. Each new action sparks a counteraction. Each cause has an effect that may then become a cause and produce a countereffect.

Cause and effect provides a highly effective structure for motivation. When a viewer sees someone initiate an action, the viewer in turn expects a counteraction. The motives of a character have force when the viewer sees why, for instance, a bad guy wants to shoot a marshal. In addition, cause-and-effect structure initiates most foreshadowing. By providing reasons for certain courses of action, what is possible becomes probable, providing suspense and coherence.

OTHER TRADITIONAL PATTERNS

Documentary and educational films (as well as their fictional cousins) adapt especially well to the traditional patterns of organizing essays. Although cause and effect is the most important nonchronological basis for organization, several other patterns appear often. Many educational films organize around problems of **definition**. The filmmaker explains and illustrates some concept by breaking it into components, explaining each, and then showing how each part contributes to the whole. Or, a filmmaker might choose to demonstrate some **process**, organizing his materials according to the necessary steps in a particular procedure. Process explains "how to." A film might show how to load film into cameras, for example. Each step of the loading would be explained in the order the procedure must be followed.

Classification and division offers yet another structure useful for explaining something. The relationship of parts to a whole serves as the primary focus in classification and division. For example, an educational film might wish to show the various types of cameras under the classification "movie cameras." The film would probably include three "divisions": 35mm, 16mm, and 8mm. Individual cameras and their operational differences would be handled under each division.

If the filmmaker wished to show similarities and differences among the cameras in one classification, he would organize by **comparison and** contrast. The basis for comparison would be, say, the handling features of various 16mm cameras. Two methods would then be available: consider one by one each camera and its features; or examine one feature at a time (such as loading the film magazine), treating each camera in relation to each feature.

Analysis and **argument** are always open to the filmmaker, as they are to the essayist. A film may examine and analyze the value of the grading system used in most schools, for instance. Or a film may be organized to argue against the grading system, producing strong arguments to make its case and defusing opposing arguments by raising and "proving" wrong all objections.

The methods used in educational and documentary films show up in fictional films as well, although fictional films tend to rely on less easily identifiable and less clearly delineated patterns of organization. **Cross-cutting** (also called **parallel editing**) is one minor technique seen frequently on the organizational levels of scenes in both fiction and documentary or educational films. Cross-cutting occurs when action on the screen switches alternately between events at one location or time to those of another. From event A, for instance, action would cut to event B and then back to A, creating a pattern of A-B-A-B-A-B-A-B. This pattern can be used in a comparison-and-contrast educational film or in a fictional film. When a marshal chases a bad guy, for instance, the camera will alternate between marshal and bad guy, creating an A-B-A-B pattern. (Writers also use cross-cutting when alternately advancing various parts of a narrative.)

Cross-cutting in fictional films creates a sense of the interplay between opposing forces. The generation of conflict can be followed from the points of view of both participants. In addition, cross-cutting allows time to be lengthened, heightening cinematic tension even further. While it might take the bad guy two minutes to run up a flight of stairs in reality, cross-cutting will allow the action to be stretched to three or four minutes while intensifying action rather than making time seem slow.

Repetition is another minor method of organization appearing on scene and sequence levels. Traditionally, repetition is one of the most common rhetorical techniques and works both to emphasize a point and as an element of organizational continuity. A character might, for example, always be filmed from a high angle, establishing both a character pattern and a way of looking at him. Another character might always be shot with clouds and sky behind him. In addition, repetition of similar hand or body movements provides an element of continuity.

But repetition can also appear in a more distinctly structural form. Each sequence might have a similar pattern with only slight variations. For example, Orson Welles and Herman Mankiewicz structured *Citizen Kane* on an interview framework. Each sequence involves a reporter seeking out someone Kane knew well and asking questions while Kane's acquaintance pauses, reflects, and then recounts some aspect of the man's life. The general structures of each sequence are very similar, with slight variations according to the personality and information of the person interviewed.

ORGANIZING THE WHOLE

A number of alternatives exist for structuring an entire film. Many fictional films, like many novels and epic poems, organize around a journey or a quest. The journey and quest both use travel as a loose binder for a series of partially related adventures and incidents. The *Odyssey* uses this episodic framework, as do the *Canterbury Tales, Tom Jones,* and *Easy Rider.* The journey, usually toward some goal, is one of the frequent organizational premises in both print and film literature.

But two other patterns must take credit for generating most movie output—the **chase** and the **peep show.** As primitive tribes described movies to Hortense Powdermaker, they go "kiss-kiss" and "bang-bang." [1] So close does this come to describing the two basic types of film action that the American film critic, Pauline Kael, has taken *Kiss Kiss Bang Bang* as the title for one of her books. "Kiss-kiss" suggests a voyeuristic look into the private lives of others. What the viewer sees is generally just beyond the pale of social respectability, but enticing for its private or forbidden quality. The **peep show** involves not only scenes of nudity and lovemaking, but also the private words and actions of people. Most television soap operas use nothing but the peep show: divorces, affairs, operations, drug use, problems with children, and every other possible pain, problem, and joy a person can privately experience.

The **chase,** on the other hand, is key to all action films. The marshal chases the bad guy, the detective pursues the criminal, the hunter tracks down the animal, and so on. Since the chase often culminates in some sort of violence, the "bang-bang" description fits nicely. Many films combine elements of both chase and voyeurism, most notably the spy-thrillers of the sixties. James Bond, for example, goes from bed to chase and back to bed. Such films exploit an audience's hunger for both adventure and forbidden fruit.

Elements of the chase and the peep show do not, however, provide precise structure in most cases. Some films, of course, organize around nothing but the chase or peep show in order to titillate and exploit emotion. Hence, skin flicks and auto races (or soap operas and quiz shows) are often two sides of the same coin. "Kiss-kiss" and "bang-bang"

[1] Roy Huss and Norman Silverstein, *The Film Experience* (New York: Harper & Row, 1968), p. 15.

represent the lowest level of pandering to audience tastes when used with no other sense of purpose than to exploit. But most films, especially good ones, organize in more complex ways, subordinating "kiss-kiss" and "bang-bang" to other purposes.

PLOT

Essays, documentaries, and the varieties of educational and propaganda films tend to be organized along traditional expository lines (definition, classification and division, comparison and contrast, and so on). Fictional films, on the other hand, normally operate within the framework of a plot, adapting in various minor ways the sorts of organizational methods mentioned above. Most feature films use plot in much the same way as novels do.

A **plot** is an organized series of interrelated events, progressing through the interplay of conflicting forces. The sources of conflict are multiple: nature, another person, society, fate, or even the divided soul of a man at war with himself (Macbeth or Dr. Strangelove, for example). A plot is a series of events that are planned in the sense that a human consciousness evolves the elements of a plot, pruning out the irrelevant. A plot is not a series of events "sliced" from life, despite occasional attempts to provide such an illusion. A filmmaker's necessary condensation of time and limitation of space require choosing which events most forcefully make a point; mundane details must be left out. A plot requires an artist to impose order upon elements found randomly in life.

The series of actions contributing to a plot contains a beginning, moves through a sensible sequence of events, and has a logical outcome. Three hours of a plane trip is not a plot unless some interconnected series of events with beginning, development, and conclusion occurs. The midsection of a plot increases tension and suspense, preparing for and building to a high point in the action. Running through each level of a plot is the unifying thread of the theme. The theme prevents actions from occurring in isolation, weaving events into a system or pattern of action.

Three types of plot can be distinguished: **plots of action, plots of character**, and **plots of idea**. Each involves elements of the other two, but the filmmaker's choice of dominant focus is highly important.

Plots of action rely mainly on the "bang-bang" elements of the chase. Such films emphasize action and movement, depicting a flurry of events in the lives of the main character or characters. Plots of action always seem to have many things happening (often simultaneously) as the situation of a protagonist changes. Change, of course, comes from conflict and from confrontation with other characters and with implied or stated ideas. The marshal chases the bad man, undergoes grueling conditions, kills the bad man, and marries the pretty shopkeeper—all in the name of goodness and justice. The viewer sees what happens from the "outside" in plots of action; motivations or nuances of character receive scant attention.

Plots of character frequently rely on the "kiss-kiss" of the peep show in the sense that the viewer witnesses the private actions and thoughts of characters. The focus in such plots is upon the process of change within characters. The change can be moral or philosophical, or it can be one of maturity or of attitude over a long period of time. In any case, the protagonist is a different person at the end from what he was at the beginning. He may kick drugs, learn that he is capable of action, learn that he cannot defy the gods, or simply be depicted as a man who has grown progressively alienated from society. Action precipitates his change, and ideas mold and play over what happens, clarifying and explaining.

Plots of idea provide mostly intellectual fare. In such plots, characters serve as representatives of various elements of an idea, and the purpose is usually philosophic statement or clarification. The characters normally represent types and hence go through almost no psychological changes. Action serves to provide physical evidence of a principle. The conflict within the protagonist is one of ideas brought on by character and action.

Few contemporary films rely on plots of idea, and most of these come from the theater. *Marat/Sade,* for example, depicts characters representing an ideological conflict rather than portraying formation and changes in private feelings and attitudes. *Dr. Strangelove* represents a film, not originating in theater, focusing on a conflict in ideas presented through surface characterization. Dr. Strangelove, the man, even has a body divided against itself. One half, with a hand gloved in black, represents forces of death and annihilation; the other half thinks primarily of mad procreation. Plots of idea tend to rely on comedy, satire, allegory, or black humor.

The peculiar synthesis of any plot requires the presence of action, character, and idea, but the dominance of one ingredient determines the nature of the plot. One element acts as the synthesizing principle. Once the dominating principle is selected, elements of plot follow. Characterization, for example, requires scenes of carefully controlled length and intensity so that the internal responses and changes of a character can be built brick by brick. Plots of idea, on the other hand, move more easily from scene to scene, but require more dialogue; such plots need to keep the eye busy while abstract points are made and reinforced. To do this, plots of idea will usually make extensive use of symbols and of settings containing suggestive meanings. Each type of plot obviously must adapt the structures of filmmaking to its own needs.

CLIMAX AND OBLIGATORY SCENE

The various types of plots rely upon conventional beginning, middle, and end structures. Beginnings set up theme and emotional climate, middles develop conflicts according to the type of plot, and ends pull everything together. Most films, however, point all action to a major climax and usually include what is called an **obligatory scene.**

Climax is one of those words everyone but the experts uses and understands. But not everyone means the same thing by the word— hence the legitimate discomfort of experts with the word. Two basic directions for climax can be distinguished: the turning point in the action, and the point of highest viewer interest and response. The first is the climax in a technical sense, while the second can more properly be regarded as the obligatory scene.

The concept of the **climax** as a turning point comes from traditional dramatic structure. According to the pattern of traditional drama, the protagonist at some time during the play makes a decision pointing the action in a clearly defined way and altering whatever course of events would have occurred without his decision. At this point, the "rising action" turns and "falling action" begins. In the sense that the action of the climax is pivotal, it reveals purpose and theme in the sharpest possible forms.

However, when most people use **climax**, they do not have in mind a turning point or decision. The moment of decision frequently occurs in an apparently calm situation. Hamlet's decision to kill King Claudius, for example, is a relatively calm climax but the high point of the play occurs at the end during the sword fight. It is the period when action is most intense that many people call climax. This action is technically called the obligatory scene.

An **obligatory scene** fulfills the expectations aroused by the conflicts and tensions within a story. As soon as he sees the marshal and the bad guy as dominant characters, for instance, a viewer knows they will inevitably confront one another. The confrontation normally takes place at the end, and throughout the movie the filmmaker heightens the viewer's anticipation of this confrontation. Anticipation and suspense are key elements in a film, and by providing minor skirmishes between warring parties a filmmaker builds tension. Imagine a viewer's disappointment (and confusion) if a major confrontation never took place. The fulfillment of scenes of intensifying action provides the viewer with a sense of release from and satisfaction with that action. James Bond must face Goldfinger just as David must meet Goliath. And the confrontation of chief characters is so momentous that the lives of both are forever changed.

Climaxes and obligatory scenes function on the level of scene and sequence as well as on the level of the whole film. The final climax and obligatory scene are by far the most important, but minor movements also contribute high points. On all levels, climaxes or obligatory scenes must have some element of surprise to be effective. While the coming of a confrontation is predictable once a viewer is aware of certain characters, a film will seem trite if the nature of the confrontation is precisely predictable. The often repeated confrontation needs to be shown in a fresh way since elements that are unexpected and unforeseen make a point most effectively.

SPACE AND TIME

Shot 1:   A man steps out of a cab; in the background a sign says "LaGuardia"

Shot 2:   An airplane in flight

Shot 3:   A man walking from a plane toward a sign saying "Welcome to Reno"

These three short shots demonstrate a filmmaker's ability to manipulate space and time. A viewer knows a New York to Reno flight takes several hours, and he knows the distance is more than two thousand miles. Yet without feeling that reality has been violated, he lets the travel time and distance slip by on the screen in a few seconds. Film obviously has a unique ability to manipulate space and time.

Time works on three levels simultaneously: real, psychological, and dramatic. On the real level a film can reproduce an almost perfect illusion of movement as it occurs in time. A man getting out of a cab will do so at the same rate he would in life. Print cannot reproduce the illusion of actual time. A sentence describing a man exiting from a cab can involve five or five hundred words and the reader can take five seconds or five minutes to read the sentence. Film reproduces the action as it appears in life, with both sound and visuals.

Time also works on a psychological level. The viewer has a subjective sense of time that the filmmaker tries to control. Psychological time works independently of clock time. Everyone knows this from personal experience: When a person is bored, depressed, or unhappy, time seems to move slowly; when he is busy and exuberant, time moves quickly. A boring lecture seems to last hours and an exciting party always seems to end soon after it starts. Abnormal mental states alter time even more. To convey his message, a filmmaker must make his film progress at a pace consistent with the ideas he presents. If a viewer grasps the message too quickly, a film will seem too slow; if action flies by more quickly than a viewer can understand it, a film will be too fast. Both extremes will weaken a film. Ideally, a viewer should be unaware of the passage of time since duration should equal content. .

The most important aspect of time, however, is dramatic. When a filmmaker uses time to bring about vivid, emotional, and striking effects, he uses dramatic time. Unless speeded up, slowed down, or reversed by mechanical processes, time is fixed within the shot and hence nondramatic in itself. But time outside the shot, as well as that altered mechanically, is fluid and flexible. The filmmaker can manipulate it in any way he wishes. Since film has no real tenses, as do verbal languages, the continuous present of time can be altered and adapted to the needs of a filmmaker.

The continuous present of time in a film progresses in a normal chronological pattern, consequently imposing a good deal of structure (especially within shots and scenes). The present sums up what has gone before and prepares the viewer for what will happen. In this sense, the dramatic time of film works much like the mind's concept of time. Even when the mind (or film) turns to the past, it is still thinking in the present.

Yet, unlike the human mind, film does not stay long in the actual present. The dramatic tools available to the filmmaker allow the normal progress of an event in time to be accelerated, slowed, or altered. The most frequent variation of the normal rhythm of time is acceleration. The three air travel shots above illustrate accelerated time. Clock time has sixty seconds to the minute; accelerated time has more than sixty seconds worth of action in a minute. A plane trip may take three hours of clock time but only five seconds of accelerated time.

Film is a highly elliptical art since it can leave out enormous amounts of material and still make sense. In life, a man would step out of a taxi, pay the driver, walk into the airport, go to the ticket counter, check his bags, and so on, finally boarding the plane. In film, any number of steps can be eliminated to accelerate time and tighten structure. Rather than follow actual events in 1, 2, 3, 4, 5, 6 fashion, film will leave out less significant actions, moving from event 1 to 3 to 5 to 11. As film art has advanced, cinema has become more and more elliptical. An audience now expects jumps between major sections of actions and understands perfectly the meaning of such jumps. From a street scene in Rome, a film can easily jump to a hotel in Tokyo. (Major jumps without transition between two apparently unrelated actions, called **jump cuts,** have become a standard method of transition.) Visual-minded modern audiences seek and find fresh structural relationship, unveiled by quick, elliptical cuts. Such cuts bring unanticipated associations and revelations.

Accelerated time can be produced by mechanical means within a shot as well. Subject motion can be increased by filming at a slower speed than normal so that normal projection rate will speed up the action. A camera can also create a sense of intensified experience by moving rapidly toward or away from a subject, approaching or retreating at a high velocity. Such increases in motion must, of course, be motivated. Otherwise, increased velocity will dizzy without informing or enlightening the viewer.

Time can be slowed down just as it can be accelerated, but decelerated time occurs less frequently. An event taking one minute can be spread out to take three minutes if the filmmaker chooses to do so. The primary method of decelerated time is the mechanical technique of slow motion. Film is run through the camera at a rate faster than normal so that it will appear slower than usual when projected. Or the camera can use slow pans, zooms, and trucking shots to create the illusion of decelerated time.

Speed can also be reduced outside of the shot. A fight lasting one minute, for example, can take three minutes if other elements receive attention at the same time. A face reacting in the crowd, another fight starting, a horse shying—any additional information helps slow down action. Repetition also allows reduced speed. Repeating an event increases the time it seems to take to occur. Or part of an event can be repeated, making a film move two steps ahead, one back, then two more ahead. In addition, short flashbacks can be used to slow time. While a character has brief thoughts flash into his mind, time is halted. (The effect does not hold for long flashbacks; they tend to move into their own continuous-present time pattern.) When such techniques are used a viewer may, however, have no psychological sense of slowed time. Ironically, the most tension-filled and seemingly rapid segment of an obligatory scene is the most likely part of a film to be slowed.

Cross-cutting (**parallel editing**) can also slow time, though it need not. Cross-cutting moves the viewer between two parallel actions. For example, one group of men might be hunting, while another goes to town for supplies. By following group A for awhile, then switching to group B, the film follows both courses of action. If all actions of both are followed, clock time will be doubled. If, on the other hand, clock time is maintained, breaches in the actions of each group will be easily recognizable. Because it juxtaposes events, cross-cutting is one of the most important editorial tools available to a filmmaker. Through cross-cutting, he can weave relationships and bring courses of action together.

Alterations in time necessarily involve alterations in space. To show a man sitting in a café reading a paper followed by a shot from a different angle would indicate no movement in time or space beyond the instant taken to cut between shots. The viewer automatically realizes that time movements involve space movements as well. The alteration of image size and light qualities on the screen represents actual movement in physical space. The visual component of film produces changes in light intensity and pattern, and these changes are taken by a viewer to mean that both space and time have changed. If the man sitting in the café were next seen walking along a forest road, for example, a viewer would assume a substantial amount of time had passed.

Film moves as freely in space as it does in time. As viewers, we sit in one place yet instantaneously the medium shifts us from spot to spot. In life our ability to draw closer to a subject, as well as our ability to change angle of vision, depends directly on the amount of time it takes to move physically from position to position. Film, on the other hand, moves us instantly from New York to Reno without disturbing our sense of reality. From a back view of a situation, we easily move to a view of only the speaker's lips. Such movements do not distort our concept of space, but enhance our understanding of content. Cinema moves freely in space and time, effortlessly doing what the mind can only dream of.

By manipulating time and space for his own purposes, a filmmaker imposes order where none exists. The chaos of man's situation can be brought under some measure of control, strengthening the ability of individual men to deal with the reality of their own situations by helping them define the world around them. If a filmmaker should refuse to reorder time and space, he would only convey chaos without meaning. Instead, a filmmaker must structure both time and space, using them as a major organizing principle. Art represents man's fight against chaos, and the filmmaker's control over time and space becomes his prime tool for raising a structure of order out of chaos.

Structure in film works simultaneously on several levels. Many organizational elements and patterns contribute to the final product. The viewer cannot expect a neat little structure of four bare walls and a roof if a film is worthwhile. He cannot simply expect to use clever little diagrams to deal with film structure, for diagrams would only mislead and subvert the beauties and complexity of structure. Instead, a viewer must realize that structures operate at all levels of a film in mutually complementary ways. A house has many different kinds of rooms, with windows, doors, closets, trim, and perhaps a fireplace. Each has its own structural principle, which has in turn been melded with the whole. One can expect no less from a film.

RHYTHM
AND CONTINUITY

Various architectural structures encourage different types of eye movement. A Gothic cathedral, for example, sweeps the eye heavenward, spiritualizing all within its bounds. Like Gothic cathedrals, films must provide rhythms and continuities that will carry the eye and the mind along the emotional and intellectual lines of a structure's development. Unlike most art forms, which cannot escape stasis, cinema depends on actual—not implied—motion and energy. Using motion and energy effectively is one of the most important tasks a filmmaker faces. But it is not the first of his tasks since a complicated process leads up to the actual release of motion and energy.

THE EDITOR'S TASK

Almost anyone can have the initial idea for a film, but it is the scriptwriter who gives a film its first form in words, shaping the product into a structured and unified whole. The director then takes the scriptwriter's words and creates a **storyboard** (also called **continuity sketches**) consisting of sketches of potential shots. The result looks much like a comic-strip. Action is broken into an ordered series of potential shots, bringing about the first step in realizing a film visually. After settings are established, the individual shots planned by the director are taken by a cameraman. Filmmakers call the lengths of footage taken during the course of filming **rushes** or **dailies**. These are uncut rolls of film taken directly from the camera and processed as the shooting of a film proceeds.

All the rushes then go to the editor, who is responsible for selecting and arranging the shots that most effectively reveal theme and purpose. Although each person along the line has a hand in shaping a film, the editor must finally make all decisions establishing the actual pace and the materials clarifying progression. He does far more than preserve the intentions of others even though he handles a film last. He also does more than correct deficiencies of script, direction, and filming. He makes a creative contribution to the realization of a film, welding hundreds of pieces of film together into a unit with a distinct rhythm and sense of order. In doing so, he contributes heavily to a film's rhetoric, since he is the one who puts things together to evoke feelings and ideas with images coordinated to achieve effects he can predict. The skill of ordering is at the very core of film rhetoric.

The editor is, however, the historical Johnny-come-lately to film. Not until the work of such Russians as Pudovkin and Eisenstein in the 1920s was the editor considered significant. At first filmmakers treated the camera as a passive witness, recording action much as a still camera does. When a film was made, someone simply put the pieces together, making sure that the order made sense.

Although the American filmmaker D. W. Griffith was among the first to understand the plasticity of film and the potentials of editing, it was the Russians who gave their full attention to editing's nuances and proselytized for this aspect of film art. Their excitement over the potential effects of editing led to the usual overstatement of those who have new ideas and want to be convinced that a new world will begin with their insight. But the impact of their ideas cannot be denied. They recognized the *artificiality* of their medium; by seeing that film was not recorded reality but artistic material capable of manipulation, they advanced the art of film. They pointed out that the filmmaker determined content, contrary to the opinions of those who considered the camera a recorder set up to capture the content in front of it. The ultimate reality of film, the Russians suggested, came from the way bits of celluloid could be chosen and arranged in relation to each other.

The editor obviously cannot structure and form an entire film in his mind. That problem belongs to the scriptwriter. But the editor must constantly make choices about the immediate action. The cumulative effect allows him extensive control over the direction and meaning of a film. At each turn of a film he selects the most persuasive vehicle for conveying an idea. In exercising choice he creates both mood and meaning.

An editor's job, however, is enormous. He faces what would seem like hopeless masses of film if one were to see all of the footage he finally throws away as well as what he includes. The size of the task explains why many films take over a year to finish, even with several people involved in the editing. The editor has no neat order to rely on at first. Films are seldom shot in chronological order—mainly for such practical reasons as money, time, and availability of locations. Instead, all shots at one location are taken at one time. For example, a western may open in a saloon, have three or four scenes in the saloon during the middle of the movie, and then end with another scene in the saloon. All saloon shots will be taken at one time. The crew will then move on to all town shots, then to all shots on the range. Some television serials even use an assembly-line method; for example, the kitchen scenes for fifteen episodes will all be filmed together during a period of several days, then backyard scenes will be shot for several days, and so on until the whole series is complete.

Obviously someone must know what he is doing in the process of filming all scenes at a location regardless of order; otherwise confusion would be rampant—and expensive. Imagine having to return to South America for one missed shot! The "someone" is the director. (Although other people, such as the producer or the script girl, take much of the burden of maintaining continuity from the director's shoulders—especially in such matters as aligning furniture properly or matching razor nicks or suntans.) Films simply do not have the continuous process of the theater when they are being made. Many actors know almost nothing of what a film is about, having little but their own parts to look at. This explains why some controversial films, such as *Citizen Kane,* can be made in secret although many people are involved. Only the writer, the director, and sometimes the major actors need to be aware of what a film is all about.

The editor must also know what the filmmaker intends, however. But the editor need not worry about the process of filming. He receives the rushes as the film is being made. Using the script as a guide, he selects the best takes and assembles a **rough cut**, much like the rough draft of a manuscript. Later he hones his product, bringing to life the **fine cut**, which is his most effective manipulation of materials. During the fine cut the editor also adds supporting material to the visuals, such as special effects, laboratory produced transitions, and the **mix** (all sounds at their proper volume levels). In short, the editor takes thousands of separate visual and aural images and assembles them into a dynamic whole.

The actual process of editing goes by several names, but usually "cutting" and "editing" are used. Little confusion results from the word **editing** since filmmakers use it chiefly to indicate the process of joining together strips of film. **Cut** and **cutting**, however, have other meanings: an individual strip of film consisting of a single shot; the separation of two pieces of action as a "transition" (used when one says "to cut to"); a verb meaning to join shots together in the editing process; or an order to end a take ("cut!"). The process of joining pieces is best called editing to avoid confusion.

CONTINUITY

The organic development of events in print literature is called the story. Film uses another word because of the inherent differences between film and print: **continuity**. This word acknowledges that visuals and sound come together in a unique way to create a narrative. The narrative line of a film cannot be adequately captured on paper; a script contains only sketchy fragments of continuity. A writer forms sentences a word at a time, evolving rhythms from an immense grab-bag of vocabulary. A filmmaker, on the other hand, cuts and pastes disparate shots together. Like a magazine collage, a film is formed from conflicting elements yoked into a unified and rhythmic whole.

The Russian filmmaker Vsevolod Pudovkin suggested that a "film is not shot, but built." His distinction is important. The process of creating continuity involves not only reproducing events, but re-creating them in a new and more vital way. Raw visual images and sounds fuse in a process that is far more than the sum of its parts. As if by magic, the editor transforms unrelated sensory experiences into a single unit so natural that a viewer cannot imagine any of the pieces missing.

The gestalt of a film develops (at a highly sophisticated level) the sensory patterns we see in daily life. Consider the following simple examples:

The dots have no connection, yet we read the dots as being more than dots: they are respectively a line, a rectangle, a circle, and a triangle on a line. The sum of the dots is only x number of dots; hence the patterns are something greater than the sum of the parts. Films do the same thing in a more complex way. A series of detailed images is more than image A plus image B plus image C. The images interrelate to form a statement.

GUIDING THE EYE

In establishing continuity, the editor does not simply replace one shot with another. Rhythms established within a shot by camera movement, sets, or actors must be maintained from shot to shot in a logical and artistic way. To be rhetorically effective, each shot must have some significance and relation to a filmmaker's central purpose. When an editor and director lead a viewer to look at something, they usually should have reasons beyond "prettiness." The details upon which a viewer focuses his eyes normally implant and reinforce a filmmaker's message.

An editor's most immediate task from shot to shot is to guide a viewer's eyes to the most important part of the screen. The composition of a shot leads a viewer to focus unconsciously on a certain spot on the screen. If the point of focus of the succeeding shot occurs on the opposite side of the screen, the shift of focal center will momentarily jar a viewer. Such shifts occur too rapidly for a typical viewer to catch them consciously; rather, he will be distanced and made uncomfortable without knowing why. If much poor eye guiding occurs he will probably walk out saying the movie was bad, but he will probably blame the actors for what is the fault of the editor.

One of the chief rules of eye-guiding is that no slight changes should occur between shots in camera angle or in image size along the same shooting line. To cut from a mid-shot to a mid-close-up or from an angle shot of ten feet to one eight feet above a person would produce a disconcerting jump with no new perspective or information. A viewer would most likely think a number of damaged frames had been removed, causing a "jump" in the film.

A viewer also unconsciously expects all shots to be taken from one side of an imaginary line through the center of action (called the **180-degree rule**). A blatant violation would seem to reverse the action. Imagine a hard-riding posse seen several times moving right to left suddenly shown moving left to right. A viewer would be temporarily confused by the sudden turnaround. A viewer becomes oriented to seeing action from a certain direction, and the lines of movement of that direction must be maintained.

Another example of maintaining movement between shots occurs when a character walks out of a door. If he exits on the left side of the screen then enters from the left in the next shot, a viewer assumes the actor is reentering the same room. But if this cut is meant as an exit from one room and an entrance to another, a viewer will be temporarily confused. The actor exiting left must enter from the right in the next shot if he is entering another room. A director normally takes precautions against such errors, but the editor must be sure that no oversights occur and the movements are consistent with a viewer's reasonable expectations.

In addition, shots promising a certain movement must fulfill their promise. The most frequent type of promised movement comes from a **look of outward regard**. If an actor sitting alone in a room hears a noise and suddenly looks left, the viewer assumes that the next shot will be through the eyes of the actor and that viewer and actor now see the same thing. A promised move to the left must be followed by the camera seeing what is on the left, or the viewer will be confused.

A **reaction shot** works in much the same way as a look of outward regard. When two people are talking and one looks at the other while he talks, the camera will cut to the face of the second actor to observe his reaction. A reaction shot cuts away from the main action to view a related minor part of what is going on. If a man strikes a horse, the following shot will show the horse's reaction. A fistfight will often include shots of spectator reaction. Such shots add information and move logically and emotionally with the dominant rhythm of the action. Maintaining such thrusts of action is the editor's primary job in cutting from shot to shot.

RHYTHM

An editor orchestrates movements from shot to shot, advancing cumulatively to a fluid expression of content and meaning. When a person controls movement he creates a rhythm. Some movements are fast, some slow, some graceful, and so on. Rhythmic movement surrounds us in life: Our hearts beat at a regular rate, our lungs inhale and exhale in a recurrent pattern, waves roll uniformly upon the shore, the tides come in and go out at predictable rates, and the cycles of days, seasons, and years go on methodically. Each rhythm contains meaning: Rapid breathing indicates exertion; a slow heartbeat suggests faintness of life; the changing seasons spell birth, maturity, old age, and death. Almost every human activity has its own peculiar rhythm.

Art capitalizes on rhythm. Even in free verse we immediately sense cadence, and traditional poetry relies on regular, predictable beats. Cinema also relies on rhythm—structuring shot, scene, and sequence in the movement of time.

Two kinds of rhythm can be traced in film: within the shot and outside the shot. A shot of a horse walking has a slow rhythm, while a shot of a running horse offers a rapid tempo. Movements within a shot have three sources: the object or character viewed, the background, or the camera. One, two, or all three can move within the shot to establish rhythms. Rhythm outside the shot resides in the measured time a shot stays on the screen. Five shots of fifty seconds each would create a slow pace, while a minute's worth of half- and three-quarter-second shots would establish an extremely rapid pace.

Usually an editor matches rhythm within and outside the shot. Shots of a leisurely walk on Sunday afternoon will be held for a long time, while shots of a fistfight will be short and rapid. Just as an excited heartbeat and respiration suggest intense activity, so does a rapid series of camera shots. By manipulating the speed at which shots occur, an editor forces a viewer to perceive meaning through kinesthetic sensation.

Rhythm of all types involves variations in speeds. Musical and poetic rhythms move regularly between strong and weak elements. The rhythms of film also depend on movement between strong and weak elements, although a steady, regular beat can be held for a short period. Analogies to a form such as music, with highly regular rhythms, can mislead a person trying to understand film rhythm. A film would obviously have difficulty appearing in 4/4 time. Rather, a filmmaker adapts rhythms to the pace of content, slowing down, speeding up, and alternating with the materials at hand. Effective tempo fits the movement of a scene. If a distinct tempo is obvious to an audience, the chances are that the tempo is wrong. Since rhythm moves us with the mood of the action, the viewer is normally almost unaware of rhythm.

An editor worries about many factors when achieving rhythm: cutting rate (the time shots last), pace of movement within the shot, dialogue timing, musical and sound tempo, and camera movement. The audience a film aims at determines the editor's rhetorical choices. If the pace of a film is too fast, the audience will become confused; if the pace is too slow, boredom and loss of attention will result. Audiences vary widely in cinematic literacy. Film buffs often complain that all films are paced too slowly, while a good many viewers find that modern films say too much for them to cope with.

Subject matter also determines an audience's maximum and minimum viewing speeds. If an audience is interested in the basic material of a film, an editor can pace a film quickly. But only the most devoted could tolerate a fast-paced film on "how to type." Similarly, if a viewer identifies with a character and feels that a movie speaks to him personally, he can move more rapidly with the flow of events. But imagine the problems of pacing for a sixty-year-old when seeing a film about the problems of a ten-year-old's first case of puppy love. Yet the sixty-year-old will probably be quicker to grasp the problems of a ten-year-old than the latter would be in understanding a situation involving an old man.

An editor is most likely to gear film speed to the "general public." Of course, the nature of that beast has changed with time. Increasing film literacy increases the pacing of films each decade. The films of the forties and fifties seem slow today, and indeed an average shot count shows that the average number of shots per hour has indeed increased steadily. Improved cinematic literacy means that recognition of shot content becomes easier and faster. Each viewer has a threshold of recognition; he takes a certain amount of time to recognize the meaning and important elements of a shot. This rate varies with the viewer according to his familiarity with the materials, but those most familiar with the film medium are able, as one would expect, to "see" faster and to integrate more efficiently what they do see.

The physical possibilities are endless for manipulating rhythm. As dialogue occurs a camera might switch between two characters at an even time interval, or it might switch as the speakers change. Or partway through a conversation the camera might switch to a closed door, return to the central character, then at shorter and shorter intervals return to the door to prepare for and heighten suspense over something about to happen.

Similarly, lines of movement help establish rhythms. A chase scene will show distances growing shorter. As the marshal nears the outlaw, the length of shots will also be shortened, intensifying anticipation. The rhythms of visual movements countering each other offer yet another way of heightening tension. The calvary riding left to right on the screen appears in imminent conflict with the Indians riding right to left. A sense of approaching conflict grows out of line direction, reinforced by decreasing shot duration as opposing forces near each other.

Each scene and sequence contains rhythms, and these build into the rhythm of the whole. Yet the rhythms of the subordinate units of a film contribute a great deal to a viewer's understanding. At the end of a sequence, a viewer can often pause to collect his thoughts. A full-length film cannot maintain a single frenetic (or slow) pace for ninety minutes. A viewer always moves through increasingly intense surges of action, but the rhythmic ebb and flow of scenes and sequences allow him periods of relative calm to collect his thoughts. Rhythm consequently provides the viewer with an emotional handrail, helping him to feel what his mind can then perceive.

TRANSITIONS

As the joiner of the pieces of celluloid making up a film, the editor relies on certain standardized devices to relate segments to each other and to the whole. Film uses a rhythm of visual punctuation marks, much as print does, both to qualify what precedes and to prepare for what follows.

The **cut** is the most common method of moving from shot to shot. One shot simply replaces another on the screen without any apparent transition, much as one word follows another in a sentence. A cut that blends shots so carefully that the switch is unobtrusive and natural is called a **match cut**. Most cuts in a film are match cuts. If continuity is instantaneously broken by an obtrusive switch, the result is a **jump cut**. Some jump cuts are unintentionally brought about through match cuts made poorly. But in recent years the jump cut has prospered, becoming a primary method of transition between scenes and even sequences. Rather than tipping off a viewer to a change in location or characters, an editor simply jumps from one action to another. For instance, a young man might dive into a pool but "land" in a bed in a hotel room. The jump cut brings dissimilar environments into sharp and instantaneous conflict, throwing both into relief and jarring the viewer's perceptions of each. The jump cut also indicates time changes in some situations, as in flashbacks and flash forwards. The jump cut suggests the rapidity with which a character's mind can jump to scenes of past or future.

Another major transitional device, the **dissolve** (also called a **lap dissolve**), is currently out of favor although still prevalent. The dissolve gradually merges two images by showing both shots simultaneously for a few seconds. As the second shot becomes stronger, the first becomes less and less visible, gradually disappearing completely. Like a paragraph or chapter division, a dissolve provides a viewer with a momentary break and a chance to collect his thoughts before going on. The break in continuity is not complete, however, since a dissolve links rather than separates like a jump cut. A dissolve may represent the passage of time, a change in location, or a psychological shift such as a flashback. Most dissolves occur between scenes rather than sequences. In the early years of films, dissolves were quite lengthy. Now they often occur so rapidly that the viewer must often look closely to be sure a transition is not a simple cut. (See Figures 9a–c.)

The **fade** is a much stronger transition than the dissolve. The fade breaks the flow of action completely by providing a blank screen. A **fade-out** shows the screen gradually dimming until it is black; the **fade-in** restores light to the screen until a bright image arrives. (Fades to white have also become popular in recent years.) Although traditionally ending both scenes and sequences, fades usually terminate sequences since they are extraordinarily strong and separating transitions. Not only does time or place distinctly change after a fade, but a viewer faces a black screen for a brief period of time as well. This break reinforces the separation of two actions. The fade is most appropriate where a narrative does not flow continuously but requires definite interruption. The fade is still a common form of ending in serious cinema, although the length of fades has shortened as cinematic literacy has increased.

Two highly mechanical forms of transition, the **wipe** and the **flip**, are almost completely out of favor although they seem to be making a comeback through use in television advertising. To envision a **wipe**, imagine wiping off a row of words on a blackboard but as you move the eraser a new set of words appears behind the eraser. This is what a wipe does with visual images. One image will "disappear" by being taken over and replaced by another image moving in a pattern across the screen. A wipe may move from left to right, top to bottom, diagonally, inward from all sides, outward from a pinpoint center like a ring of ripples from a thrown pebble, in a spiral, and so on. The possibilities are almost infinite.

The **flip**, on the other hand, shows an image flipping as if someone turned over a coin or a playing card. One cinematic image replaces another as if the second were the flip-side of the first. However, the flip and the wipe are patently artificial and thus call attention to themselves. They show up primarily where the filmmaker seeks a comic, antique, or stylized effect.

The **iris** is a distant—and even less popular—cousin of the wipe. The iris gradually darkens an image in a circular pattern from the edge of the frame until only a peephole remains visible. In the early days of the movies, the iris worked much like a close-up or a zoom by focusing attention on a small part of the action such as a face. Frequently the iris then blacked out the entire screen, producing an effect much like a fade. Or, a shot often opened with an iris to focus attention on one element and then expanded to reveal the full scene. Modern filmmakers use lenses to do what the iris once did, and its use is now mainly comic.

However, a stepchild of the iris, the **mask**, is still used. A mask darkens certain areas of the screen for optical effects. For example, a mask produces the illusion of a periscope, keyhole, telescope, binoculars, knothole, or a chink in a wall. The mask, however, is not intended as a transition but as an element of continuity. (Sometimes a filmmaker will mask an entire image to increase the vertical or the horizontal line, or for some other effect.)

Although modern editors no longer use many of the old standard transitions, they have come up with some of their own in addition to the jump cut. The **swish pan** blurs details by sending the camera spinning on its vertical axis. The blurred highlights and swishing movement create a rushing sensation, propelling action from one setting to another. The swish pan can also be used to suggest confusion and to intensify violent action.

The **split-screen** can also (loosely) be considered a form of transition (and is currently the rage among experimental filmmakers). Split-screen offers two or more frames of action simultaneously, with the multifaceted action interrelated by juxtaposition. The viewer's eyes are left to move from screen to screen, participating in the process of transition and able to operate somewhat independently of a filmmaker's direction. Telephone conversations, for example, are often simulated with split-screen, allowing a viewer to choose when to observe the speaker's face and when to watch the listener's reactions.

One last transitional device, the **focus-through** (or "racking"), is largely a product of modern lens technology. With a shallow depth of field, a filmmaker can use focus to achieve a transition between centers of action within a shot (or through the illusion of being within a shot). For example, a character will be in focus in the foreground with the background out of focus because of a shallow field. The cameraman will then change the focus from the first character to some previously blurred and unrecognizable character or activity in the background. The effect is much like a dissolve, but the realization that both activities were always present causes each to be read in a new light.

MONTAGE

The editor's manipulation of time and space provides cinema with its most unique artistic and rhetorical potentials. The editor imbues with meaning the raw sights and sounds of reality. But editing takes two principal forms. The first we have examined above and called "editing," explaining that it involves the artistic and rhetorical ordering of images and sounds in rhythms evoking a film's theme and movements. But another element of editorial art is no less significant: montage.[1]

Montage can perhaps be understood most easily through the Japanese hieroglyphs pointed out by Sergei Eisenstein, the initial spokesman for creative montage. The Japanese hieroglyph is a form of picture writing welding together two representative symbols. The combination of the two creates a larger meaning than can be accounted for by the sum of the two added together. One should visualize a multiplication sign between the two symbols rather than an addition sign; hence a series of images operates on the mind not by $A + B = C$ but by $A \times B = Y$. Each symbol alone represents an object; together they suggest a concept. Here are some examples from Japanese hieroglyphics:

water $\times$ eye $=$ to weep
mouth $\times$ bird $=$ to sing
dog $\times$ mouth $=$ to bark
knife $\times$ heart $=$ sorrow
mouth $\times$ child $=$ to scream

When symbols for water and eye are yoked together, for example, they mean more than eye and water; they suggest the concept of weeping with all of its implications of sorrow. The idea of weeping is not in any way built into symbols for eye or water but rather the idea of weeping emerges from the junction of the two symbols.

---

[1] The distinction between editing and montage goes by other names as well, chiefly "continuity editing" or "narrative montage" (editing) and "dynamic editing," "expressive montage" or "conditional montage" (montage). Those who speak of narrative and conditional montage have simply adopted the French word for editing, "montage." I have kept the word "montage" for the unique juxtapositional principles of editing growing out of Eisenstein's work.

Montage in film is a rhetorical arrangement of juxtaposed shots. The combination, or gestalt, produces an idea by combining the visual elements of two dissimilar images. A longing face, for instance, juxtaposed to a turkey dinner suggests hunger. Or the image of a fox following that of a man making a business deal would indicate slyness. Segments of film working together to create a single idea have no counterpart in nature; their juxtaposition occurs through the editor's imaginative efforts. Because it depends on the editor's ability to yoke dissimilar images together into a single image, montage is a highly creative form of editing.

A print counterpart to montage can be seen in the poems of the so-called metaphysical poets of the seventeenth century, especially those of John Donne. The metaphysical conceit sparks the reader's recognition by pointing out unsuspected similarities in apparently unrelated images. The result, as in film montage, is both intellectual and emotional in force. Look, for example, at the strong images of Donne's "A Valediction Forbidding Mourning," especially the final comparison of two lovers to the legs of a compass:

> As virtuous men passe mildly away,
>   And whisper to their soules, to goe,
> Whilst some of their sad friends doe say,
>   The breath goes now, and some say, no.
>
> So let us melt, and make no noise,
>   No teare-floods, nor sigh-tempests move,
> T'were prophanation of our joyes
>   To tell the layetie our love.
>
> Moving of th'earth brings harmes and feares,
>   Men reckon what it did and meant,
> But trepidation of the spheares,
>   Though greater farre, is innocent.
>
> Dull sublunary lovers love
>   (Whose soule is sense) cannot admit
> Absence, because it doth remove
>   Those things which elemented it.
>
> But we by a love, so much refin'd,
>   That our selves know not what it is,
> Inter-assured of the mind,
>   Care lesse, eyes, lips, and hands to misse.
>
> Our two soules therefore, which are one,
>   Though I must goe, endure not yet
> A breach, but an expansion,
>   Like gold to ayery thinnesse beate.
>
> If they be two, they are two so
>   As stiffe twin compasses are two,

Thy soule the fixt foot, makes no show
  To move, but doth, if th'other doe.

And though it in the center sit,
  Yet when the other far doth rome,
It leanes, and hearkens after it,
  And growes erect, as that comes home.

Such wilt thou be to mee, who must
  Like th'other foot, obliquely runne.
Thy firmnes makes my circle just,
  And makes me end, where I begunne.

The mental process the reader goes through juxtaposing images of lovers
to compass images is analogous to the way film juxtaposes images. By
joining supposedly conflicting and unrelated images, Donne forcefully
makes the point that "absence makes the heart grow fonder." (It should
be noted, however, that such an easy restatement of the poem's central
idea quite obviously fails to convey the complexity and subtlety of what
Donne is able to say through a combination of images.)

Eisenstein thought that film continuity should advance through a
series of shocks and conflicts. It does, of course, advance through progressions of conflict, but not simply the narrow conflicts of clashing then
fusing images. Most films advance chiefly through match editing; montage operates at specific times for specific effects. Even Eisenstein sparingly
used the vital clashing montage he espoused. Some of his montage
developments, though, show his ideas can be applied with great force.
In one film he juxtaposes shots of workers being gunned down and
oxen being slaughtered; in another he compares Kerensky (the Russian
prime minister overthrown by the Bolshevik Revolution in 1917) to a
peacock. Yoking such images brings about rhetorically effective comments
on political issues dear to Eisenstein and the Russians.

Eisenstein's ideas of montage continue in modern films, although
generally used more subtly today. For example, a series of shots of
women talking in a store, on a street corner, and in a beauty parlor can
create the idea of "rumor." Or the words of a president saying "we seek
only peace" juxtaposed to a shot of a bomber dropping its load on a
village creates the idea of "credibility gap" or hypocrisy.

More frequently, though, montage occurs through simple contrasts.
For example, shots of a lavish home complete with swimming pool and
servants juxtaposed to a tenement family's squalor says more than images
of squalor alone could say. Together the images point up a strong contrast and disparity of living situations with inevitable political and moral
consequences. Yet no such consequences result from simply showing
images of rich people.

One last highly effective example of montage in Orson Welles's

Citizen Kane deserves note. In a series of shots Kane and his wife are seen sitting at breakfast over a number of years. Each shot represents a passage in time, and each shows the couple sitting farther and farther apart at a progressively longer and more distancing table. At first the backgrounds are simple and the two talk lovingly. With each shot the couple talks less, the background grows more ornate and cold, and finally the two icily ignore each other with the wife reading the newspaper rivaling Kane's own *Inquirer*. The shots last only a few seconds, but the montage speaks cogently of the dissolution of a marriage.

The current development of split-screen images opens up new possibilities for montage. Juxtaposed images can be viewed simultaneously rather than sequentially. At the same time, split-screen deprives the filmmaker of an element of control. The viewer can make connections the filmmaker might not intend, or a person's optical meanderings—almost unavoidable when multiple images are present—might cause him to miss something the filmmaker considers highly important. (Potential problems, though, lie less in the technique than in the filmmaker's inability to control the rhetoric of his creation.)

Montage shows up in modern film in a few other important mechanically realized ways. **Double exposures (superimpositions)** screen two images simultaneously, causing each to comment upon the other and often evoking an idea more significant than its two parts. (Figures 9a–c.) The extraordinarily rapid pacing of images in some films also becomes montage at times. When the eye is exposed to several images per second (or even to one or two per second), the mind cannot operate upon all images in a sequential fashion. Hence the images clash and jar, generating ideas rapidly (if the viewer is not blinded first).

All principles of montage apply to sound and to sound counterpointed to visuals, as well as to visuals alone. Sounds not only reinforce, but can also generate ideas. The essence of visual montage is counterpoint—apparently unrelated images pressed up against each other and welded together to form a new unit. Sounds can also counterpoint each other and the accompanying visuals. Consider, for example, the face of the president speaking with apparently intense sincerity, but the only sounds are of hysterical shrieking and moaning. Either the visual or the sound in its proper context would make one kind of sense, but joining unrelated sights and sounds generates an entirely new idea and forces the audience to see new relationships. The most effective sound is usually that which counterpoints visuals since every bit of music, dialogue, or sound that is inconsistent with its accompanying visual image forces a viewer to use his imagination and to think about what he sees.

As with other film techniques, effective montage does not call attention to itself. The editor does not want the viewer to say, "Hey, that's montage!" Such a reaction would destroy the rhetorical effectiveness of the editor's gambit. But montage is a highly important implement in the editor's rhetorical toolbox. Effective montage speaks urgently to both the mind and emotions of the viewer.

Montage contributes one highly important element to the overall stylistic thrust of a film. At each step in the realization of a film, a scriptwriter, a director, or a cameraman adds elements to the total development.[2] And each contribution adds to the final style since style depends on subject and structure as well as on shot choice and tempo. But the final responsibility for style is in the hands of the editor because he establishes the rhythm and continuity that play upon a viewer's intellect and emotions. The editor is the person who most consciously asks questions about the rhetorical effect of each image and sound, and then puts them all together to move an audience.

---

[2] Of course, many directors do their own scriptwriting and editing, allowing complete control over the final product and hence full freedom for each director to establish his own style.

Fig. 9a.   Industrial pollution.

Fig. 9b.   A seagull.

Fig. 9c. A *double exposure* welding two unrelated images together and creating an idea from the fusion. In a *dissolve* one image merges with another for a brief double exposure, then the second image becomes dominant until it alone can be seen.

EXTENDED RHETORIC

CONNOTATION AND DENOTATION

If you were five feet tall and weighed two hundred pounds, which of the following words would you use to describe your physique: fat? cornfed? overweight? chunky? corpulent? chubby? plump? large? obese? blubbery? fleshy? stout? portly? pudgy? rotund? Which words would hurt your feelings the most?

All of the above words describe the same physical condition—an excess of flesh. The literal meaning of a word is called its **denotation**. All of the words above are synonyms of "fat," and hence have almost identical denotations when used to describe fatness. Obviously some words, such as "cornfed," can have different denotations when used to apply to other matters, but even when a word refers to two or more things the denotations remain tied to specific meanings.

Connotation, on the other hand, involves the cluster of associations or implications a word carries with it. The words above denoting "an excess of flesh" have widely varying resonances, causing people to respond to each in a unique way. Most words carry emotional overtones, and writers and speakers use these for rhetorical ends. Some connotations may be private; for example, most people have differing emotional responses to particular given names—such as Jack, Perry, Marjorie, or Phyllis— usually conditioned by acquaintances with those names. Or a group of people might have the same response to a word; for example, "America" and "hamburger" have a strong, positive connotation for most Americans, Some words, on the other hand, have connotations held in common by almost all people; light, for instance, connotes insight and clarity.

Connotations fall along a spectrum running from ameliorative (positive) to pejorative (negative). Emotionally neutral words do, of course, exist; "a," "of," "the," and "as" exemplify neutral words. But most words with any importance or spirit tend toward one pole or the other. If not already ameliorative or pejorative, words are pushed toward one or the other by context. The various choices for "fat" listed above could be spread out on such a spectrum, although most would end up on the pejorative side.

So far "denotation" and "connotation" have been considered in relation to words. But everything said about both applies to film images as well. Like words, film images are fundamental units of composition capable of emotional coloration in themselves or by the context in which they appear. Most of our discussions dealing with such matters as lighting and camera angle have revealed how a filmmaker uses technique to imbue his images with emotional impact. As these techniques have been explained, each has been considered in its variations from some sort of "norm." As a shot departs from a normative angle or position, emotional overtones increase. The more a person is literally looked down upon, the more he is figuratively looked down upon. Revealing the rhetorical methods a filmmaker uses to control connotation has been the chief aim of this book.

Denotation, on the other hand, has been implied in discussions of the "norms" of film. The denotative content of most images should be obvious since a viewer can see that a shot of a balloon means "balloon" or a shot of a man walking means "man walking." But in some instances denotative meanings can create puns as in verbal languages. A pun can be a play on either two words similar in sound but with different spellings ("sons raise meat" or "sun's rays meet") or on a single word with two incongruous but pertinent denotations ("bit"—a piece, or an act of biting). Film can use denotative images to produce visual puns similar to those occurring in verbal language. Crossed sticks of wood can indicate a telephone pole or a cross—or both. Or the filmmaker can pun with something the viewer already knows as Luis Buñuel does in *Viridiana* by arranging beggars in a banquet parodying daVinci's portrait of the Last Supper. (*M*A*S*H* similarly parodies the Last Supper through a visual pun.) By juxtaposing or implying similarity in images a filmmaker can pun, both as a device of comedy and as a tool for serious parody.

IRONY

A filmmaker can also create dual meanings in intense and sustained ways. Irony occurs when a filmmaker expresses his ideas in images suggesting the opposite of the meaning he intends. Film most frequently uses irony by counterpointing visual and aural images. Imagine, for example, "We Shall Overcome" sung in juxtaposition to images of policemen beating black people, or images of a tenement family's apartment set against the sounds of a debutante ball.

Two types of irony can usually be distinguished in film—rhetorical and dramatic. **Rhetorical irony**, the most common variety, advocates attitudes opposite to those literally expressed. A film might, for instance, praise the value of war as a way of population reduction, but the real message is that war harms innocent people. The filmmaker tries to make the viewer react against the surface message. **Dramatic irony,** on the other hand, occurs when the words or actions of a character suggest a meaning unperceived by him but understood by the viewer. If an event occurs in the background that the audience sees but some character does not—for example, two women gossiping about a neighbor with the neighbor secretly overhearing the conversation—irony results. In addition, an audience's prior knowledge can set up dramatic irony; such irony would occur in a film showing Hitler's promise to the German people of great victory when the viewer knows from historical fact that he failed to win his "great victory."

PARADOX

On occasion, film also utilizes **paradox**, a statement that' seems contradictory but is true. The primary rhetorical purpose of paradox is to attract attention and hence to provide emphasis. By clipping through time and space, film can, for example, have one person seem to be in two places. To give a rather obvious technical example, two newsmen can appear together on the television screen yet be thousands of miles apart. The two cannot be "together" since they are far apart, but they are together nevertheless. Similarly, two characters can be in separate cities but be "looking" at each other. The viewer sees them as if they were responding to one another. Paradoxically, they are together while apart.

IMAGERY

Although both words and visual images are tools of communication, each specializes in conveying certain kinds of information. An explanation of a philosophical system, such as Existentialism, can most easily be achieved with verbal language. High levels of abstract thought can be most economically conveyed with words. Description, on the other hand, works best when captured directly on film. Ten slow pages of descriptive information translated into visuals can be absorbed by a film viewer in seconds.

But most units of communication lie between the theoretical poles of chimerical abstraction and raw physical detail. Many sentences rely on images created like snapshots in a viewer's mind; and most film images, by their very selection, contain abstract statement as well as physical detail. Hence any simple delineation of what either medium can do must be met with a degree of skepticism.

It took a long time for both film viewers and filmmakers to realize the ability of film's imagery to extend beyond literal reproduction. And too often people still attempt to regard a film image as simply the physical conveyance of an observable phenomenon. Such people treat film images and literary images as if they were totally different entities. A literary image is not only important for the mental picture associated with it, but for the range and power of its implications and applications. Consider Marlowe's description of Helen of Troy:

> Was this the face that launch'd a thousand ships,
> And burnt the topless towers of Ilium?

The reader recognizes not only the simple images, but their complex interplay and implications as well. But can film images be as significant and as suggestive?

Film frequently strains to make images more than reproductions, just as writers strain to make written expression more than flat abstraction. As Robert Richardson suggests, ". . . one might say that literature often has the problem of making the significant somehow visible while film often finds itself trying to make the visible significant."[1] But film images have become more complex with greater audience sophistication. More and more frequently, one must give his full attention to sort through and grasp the implications of film imagery.

A great many filmmakers tie their images to single meanings or associational values. The collection and use of literal images in a film is obvious, and such images are as important to a filmmaker's lexicon as abstract words are to a writer. But most filmmakers also construct interesting and evocative images with widely ranging associations and implications. These images, providing insight and clarification, function much like literary tropes and are almost as important to film as they are to verbal languages. A **trope** (also called a figure of speech in verbal languages) "turns" or alters the sense in which an audial or visual image is used in film. The image takes on more meaning than its physical

[1] *Film and Literature* (Bloomington, Indiana: Indiana University Press, 1969), p. 68.

configuration alone suggests, just as a cross means more than one stick of wood nailed to another.

METAPHOR

The most important film trope is **metaphor**. As in verbal languages, a film metaphor is an implied analogy linking one image to another and associating qualities of one with the other. The two halves of a metaphor are called *tenor* and *vehicle*. The tenor is the primary subject or idea, and the vehicle is the image used to comment upon the subject or idea. In a metaphor from Charlie Chaplin's *Modern Times,* a shot of a crowd of people emerging from a subway becomes the tenor while the following shot of a herd of moving sheep is the vehicle. The metaphor conveys the idea that people in the city are like sheep.

Almost all shot comparisons can be called metaphors since all cinematic comparisons are implicit while also being direct. Film does not say "X is like Y" or "an analogy to R is M," although educational films will occasionally include verbal similes or analogies. Most films, on the other hand, do not "point out" comparisons but juxtapose images directly, leaving the viewer to perceive applications. When a metaphor becomes too obvious, it loses force or becomes comical. If included in a serious contemporary film, the sheep metaphor from *Modern Times* would probably seem too obvious or trite.

Because effective film metaphors tend to be highly subtle, the point at which an image becomes a metaphor is tenuous. If a filmmaker juxtaposes visual images of a Joint Chiefs of Staff meeting to audial images of a pack of howling hounds on a chase, the metaphor is obvious. But when a filmmaker shows a man and woman fondly looking at each other and then cuts to such nature images around them as wind moving the grass, trees blowing, and flowers newly bloomed, the metaphor becomes more subtle. Most film metaphors work to evoke feelings in the viewer, chiefly by helping him to relate remembrances and associations from his own life to experiences handled on the screen. Hence metaphors for love, fear, kindness, and so on must evade the viewer's conscious note that "this is a metaphor" while touching the quick of his spirit. The viewer then becomes emotionally (and sometimes intellectually) aware that one thing is like another by seeing the two side by side, but he does not reduce either to a simplistic "X is like Y."

Because love is a prime film topic and because our society still largely disapproves of showing the physical act of love on the screen (there are often good esthetic reasons not to do so as well), the most common screen metaphors depict the act and climax of lovemaking. Even though meant as alternatives for showing the "real thing," the visual substitutes become actual metaphors for passion. The list of metaphors for lovemaking could go on and on, but a few will make the point: waves advancing and retreating on the shore; jets of fluid; rain beating with increasing intensity against window panes, then abating to a slow trickle of droplets; trees blown by increasingly intense winds, finally yielding to calm; flames leaping then subsiding; planes refueling in midair; oil pumps at work; rapid forward tracking shots, intensifying then stopping. Even given contemporary "permissiveness" such metaphors still occur frequently since a metaphor allows a denser and more allusive statement than the literal image alone could convey. In every case, the image of the vehicle carries out the idea of the tenor.

Occasionally a filmmaker will realize an extended metaphor that can in turn become a structuring element. For example, in *Mother* Vsevolod Pudovkin parallels the Russian masses to a river. Their inactivity suggests a frozen river; as their indignation begins, the river starts to thaw, melting more rapidly as their indignation turns to wrath; as they move to action and rebellion, the river breaks up sending chunks of ice destructively downstream.

Metaphors are inherently illogical; a person compares two things having no natural relationship. Yet in an effective metaphor the vehicle throws light upon the tenor by forcing a viewer to consider similarities between the two. By seeing unlike qualities held side by side, a viewer sees a problem in a fresh way.

In constructing metaphors, cinema has one distinct advantage over verbal language: It can use verbal language *and* film language. Metaphors can be constructed from a montage of sound plus sound, visual plus visual, or sound plus visual. From the counterpointing and juxtaposing of montage grows effective cinematic metaphor. The whole becomes much greater than the sum of its parts.

SYMBOL

Symbols are another type of film trope, although they are not necessarily created by montage. Unlike metaphors, symbols *embody* an idea or quality. A metaphor, on the other hand, uses an image with few intrinsic associations as an analogy to illustrate and clarify an idea or quality. The same image used in a different situation will take on another meaning. A symbol, however, evokes a network of interrelated meanings and is used consistently in the same way. A symbol calls forth a level of meaning beyond what can be found in immediate detail.

Like print symbols, film symbols come in two varieties—those with universal or widely agreed-upon meanings and those with meaning generated within a work. Symbols with widely agreed-upon meanings appear both in real life and in works of art. For example, a circle suggests continuity and endlessness and is found in such forms as the wheel, the wedding band, and the mandala. Some symbols are universal among cultures, such as water, while others are agreed upon by members of a culture or subculture, such as a flag, a cross, a swastika, or a particular flower. Symbols with agreed-upon meanings appear frequently in films, often all too obviously. Who fails to groan when he sees the cross and Christ figure in yet one more movie about an alienated hero (or antihero)?

Although universal symbols can be handled with great subtlety, the most effective film symbols generate within a film to fulfill a particular rhetorical need. A few actual examples will best make the point. Sergei Eisenstein opens *Potemkin* with shots of boiling borscht intercut with inhuman working conditions that will eventually lead the crew to rebellion. The boiling borscht symbolizes the increasing agitation of the crew, which eventually leads to rebellion. In *Citizen Kane* Welles makes Kane's castle, "Xanadu," a symbol of the character of Kane: greedily rich, large and dominating, but hollow and cavernous. A filmmaker can create symbols from anything capable of being photographed, imbuing an object with meaning by the associations gradually built into it.

ALLUSION

Both metaphor and symbol try to make an image into something more dense and pervasive than it is on the surface. They extend the meaning of an image by increasing its associations. Extension of meaning can also be achieved within individual shots through **allusion**, an indirect reference to figures or events outside of the film. If the dashing marshal calls the bad guy a "Judas," the marshal alludes to the Biblical Judas with all of the traditional evil associated with him.

Most allusions tend to be verbal, but visual allusions add depth to a film as well. A camera may play upon a record album, by Elvis Presley for example, to say something about a character as well as to date him chronologically or psychologically. In a film made in the 1970s, a poster showing Humphrey Bogart can help alert a viewer to the fantasies of a character. Or an object may simply appear in the frame and require the viewer to be on the lookout for implications. For example, a painting by Picasso, such as "Guernica," would allude to the destructiveness of war and contain significance for certain films. The casual objects found within a film's visuals frequently enlarge meaning by pointing to important events with which the viewer is likely to be familiar.

Filmmakers sometimes play games with allusions, either challenging with allusions difficult to grasp or by inserting private jokes. In filming *The Magnificent Ambersons,* Orson Welles included a scene with one character reading the same paper (*The Enquirer*) that the character Charles Foster Kane published in Welles' *Citizen Kane,* the film preceding *Ambersons.* This sort of allusion provides fun and games for film buffs, but tells the audience little. Nor are private "in-jokes" helpful when the filmmaker expects only a handful of "in" people to catch on.

Allusions are useful only if a viewer with reasonable sophistication can spot them. Traditional allusions are, of course, fairly safe. But some allusions get lost with time because they are topical. A reference to Ann Dvorak (who was an American leading lady of the 1930s) would be meaningless in most instances, just as an allusion to the rock group *The Union Gap* would mean nothing in twenty years except to a small segment of the population with a good memory. Allusion that is grasped, though, genuinely extends meaning.

HYPERBOLE AND UNDERSTATEMENT

Hyperbole is a trope using conscious exaggeration to achieve emphasis or create a comic effect. Hyperbole is brought about by exaggerating action at some phase of production, from the mechanics of the camera to acting and sets. Fast motion, for example, is a chief device for hyperbole, usually creating a comic sense of frenzy. Or music may be modulated (changed in intensity), swelling to excessively thunderous levels to drive home a point. Occasionally actors exaggerate movements, especially the strong movements of the stage that appear too emphatic and stylized for film, or assume countenances with unmistakably strong emotions. Most comedy, especially slapstick, relies on hyperbole. Anything from an actor's clothing to his attempt to climb a ladder can be exaggerated.

Hyperbole treated in a serious way creates **emphasis**. Normally films handle emphasis by consciously manipulating the mechanical aspects of filming. For example, a shot will be held "too long" or it will be repeated. The freeze-frame provides yet another method of emphasis by fixing an image amid a flux of movement. Masking devices also establish emphasis by concentrating a viewer's attention on a particular area of the screen. Even the simply dollying or zooming in on an object or expression provides emphasis. But there is clearly a line (a fine one, to be sure) between emphasis and hyperbole; all hyperbole creates emphasis, but not all emphasis is hyperbolic. Focusing attention on an object is not in itself hyperbolic but emphatic, yet emphasis becomes hyperbole when a shot is held a few seconds longer or repeated one more time.

The functions of hyperbole—humorous effect or emphasis—are also those of **understatement**, although understatement is especially adaptable to satire while hyperbole mainly provides a bed for raucous humor. Understatement can be achieved through camera technique as well as through acting or setting. Cutting short an obviously significant image, for instance, arouses a viewer's curiosity. Hence understatement contributes a great deal to the suspense (and fear) of mystery or horror movies. By not seeing quite enough and by being tantalized, a viewer finds his apprehensions growing. Similarly, humor or satire can be created or intensified by underplaying or slowing an image, as when a man slipping on a banana peel is shown in slow motion.

PERSONIFICATION

Personification works in a more literal and obvious way in film than in literature. Personification is a trope endowing animals, abstractions, or inanimate objects with human form or character. Something nonhuman takes on human personality, intelligence, and emotions. Most film personification obviously occurs in cartoons, with characters such as Mickey Mouse or the Road Runner taking on human attributes. But personification also works in nonanimated films. A haunted house can seem human in its dealings with inhabitants, or a dog such as Lassie can be given the flatulent moral values of a huckster preacher. By carefully building relationships from shot to shot, a filmmaker can endow anything nonhuman with human qualities.

ACTING

Film acting usually receives scant attention, and this book is no exception. The subject seems capable of being handled on only two levels: as a full study in itself designed primarily for actors, or as a minor aspect of the overall process of film. When a book on film focuses on cinema's broad range of styles, methods, and approaches, acting blurs into the background while the intricate problems of film mechanics dominate. Although the actor is obviously a highly important (and absolutely necessary!) contributor to a film, it is more difficult to be specific about the hows and whys of his rhetorical contribution. Acting cannot be considered in isolation and must be examined in the light of direction and editing. After all, an actor is under the control of his director at every turn, and after every scene an actor's whole performance yields to the slicing of the editor's scissors.

Several elements make the process of film acting unique and at odds with the demands of the stage. Perhaps most important of all, the film actor does not enjoy the encapsulated continuity of the stage actor. The stage actor knows that after two or three hours he can go home, put his feet up, and turn on the TV knowing that his job has been completed. He puts on a complete and self-contained performance. He develops a role from the opening of a play through all of the rising and falling action until the conclusion. The screen actor, on the other hand, works in noncontinuous bits. Each acting stint is not much longer than the length of a shot, usually less than a minute. All day long, day after day, the screen actor must produce and reproduce one brief bit after another. He never knows a developed, sustained performance.

Nor can the screen actor rely on continuity in his daily grind. In one day he may have to act out parts from a film's beginning, middle, and end, or he may spend the first week's shooting doing nothing but the final moments of a film. The physical needs of cinema require that all shots at a particular location be taken at one time. A director cannot fly his crew to Bombay and back three times just to follow script chronology. When all cameras, equipment, and props are set up in one location, the director must complete all shots at that place before moving on. This puts unusual strain on an actor since he cannot grow with a part but must be instantly ready to evoke any phase of a devoloping and changing character's personality.

The conditions of filming also affect an actor. He works amid a busy set with technicians and other actors watching him, but without a real audience. The separation of an actor from a live audience makes his task even more difficult. A live audience provides an actor with a barometer—he can judge (and alter) his performance according to audience response. He also feels reinforcement when an audience responds to his efforts and establishes sustaining emotional resonances with the people in front of him. The film actor must do everything for the camera that a live audience expects, yet he faces only the unblinking stare of the lens and the people who happen to be on the set during a take.

The penetrating and unforgiving eye of the camera provides the film actor with one of his greatest challenges. He has no blank side, nor can he conceive of acting in relation to a defined actor-camera distance. At times the camera will be fifty feet from him and at times it will be only inches away. In addition, he knows that distance does not necessarily reduce his image size since the filmmaker can switch among lenses of varying focal lengths. When the camera moves in close, he must treat it as something almost animate, realizing that its eye will see and record any false move or insincere gesture, destroying a take. The camera will not allow him to be out of character for even an instant. So revealing is the camera eye that an actor must become one with the character he represents or the camera will shout "liar!"

Early film acting carried over techniques from the stage. Today we laugh at the exaggerated mannerisms seen in very old films—mannerisms that were successful when audiences were less sophisticated and were kept at respectable theater distance because filmmakers possessed only a single lens of standard focal length. Gradually, however, film actors developed their own style. Film acting now requires great subtlety and restraint. A small movement of a lip conveys enormous content in a close-up, but if an actor makes a quiver of his lip too obvious the action will become comical. Every slight movement of face or body comes under the unforgiving scrutiny of the camera's eye, and an actor must be sure that each nuance of movement "explains" a facet of character.

Motivation is even more important in film than in drama since film deals with intensified emotions in a more sustained fashion than does drama. A script provides basic motivations, and an actor must be aware of the scope of motivation at each stage of a film. Cinema places an actor in direct relationship with his environment, and he must react to the clues that grow out of his surroundings. Not only must an actor deliver his lines convincingly, but he must be able to visualize forcefully his emotional state through the miming expressions of face and body.

Many filmmakers have a "noble savage" concept of film actors, believing that amateurs have an innate sense of what they actually do in life and hence offer very convincing screen presences. A great many films have indeed made successful use of amateurs. But such films rely heavily on editing, taking essentially expressionless faces and defining their feelings by context. An audience then reads in expressions from the montage.

Amateur actors are not especially useful when the complexities within a character must be made visual; rather, amateurs most effectively show "types" at work (the fisherman, the welfare recipient, the sports reporter and so on). In addition, amateur actors have difficulties acting out even their most common daily rituals since a camera changes circumstances and responses by its very presence. Turn on a home-movie camera and everyone instantly becomes self-conscious. With a professional crew looking on, the effect can be multiplied. A savings and loan president, for example, can hardly carry out even his normal duties of interviewing and appraising when lights are glaring and cameras whirring.

One last aspect of film acting needs mention. Many actors bring a whole character and style to each role they play. Such actors do not really act in the sense that they enter different types of consciousness and then project these consciousnesses to an audience. Such actors instead only vary slightly a given personality type and play this type in role after role. John Wayne always plays John Wayne, and Humphrey Bogart always plays Humphrey Bogart. The personality actor plays roles tailored for him. And even when he might try to portray another personality, he still must combat all of the associations his audience has with his usual persona.

SENSORY PARTICIPATION

In many ways print is an aberrant literary form. As a broadly based artistic form, print did not come into its own until well after the development of printing presses in the fifteenth century. Literature, however, has a long and rich oral tradition that makes print look like a Johnny-come-lately to art. Not only was drama an oral form, but poetry and stories were passed down from bard to bard, partly committed to memory and partly adapted spontaneously to set verse patterns. Long before the *Odyssey* and *Iliad* were recording in writing they formed part of the body of Greek epic literature. Literature is consequently an entity independent of the medium within which it appears. T. S. Eliot's reading of *The Waste Land* is as much (perhaps more) a piece of literature when chanted as when set down on pages of paper.

Print, then, is an adopted child of literature only a few hundred years old in its broad artistic impact, while literature has flourished in other forms for thousands of years. In a very real sense, cinema returns us to a method of perceiving literature through sensory means—the method that dominates art. The sensory apprehension of literature extends and deepens understanding for it relies on very basic rhetorical techniques relating speaker or actor to audience. The term "rhetoric" perhaps applies better to film than to writing since rhetoric as a study was formulated before the widespread use of print and specifically focuses on audial and visual communication. The technical apparatus of cinema has, of course, vastly extended the rhetorical methods set down by the Greeks over two thousand years ago.

Rhetoric began as a study of the ways the senses of sight and hearing could be adapted to communication. It might seem strange that other senses have been neglected: taste, smell, and touch. Indeed, some people are eager to include such sensory elements in the cinematic experience. Attempts have been made to provide accompanying odors—by channeling smells through heating systems, for example—though none of these experiments has met with much success. A sensation of imminent "touch" has been achieved through three-dimensional film. As a grade-school student, I remember fearfully ducking when a native threw a spear right out of the screen; later I reached out to touch the heroine's outstretched hand. Perhaps some day a theater will hand out a "roast-beef tablet" or a "lobster tab" that the viewer can pop in his mouth at the right time.

The truth, though, is that such sensory devices have little to do with art. We can gulp reality in reality, but we look to art for other things. Touch, taste, and smell are simply not well suited for artistic communication, but are tied to and dependent on their own circumstances—and on sight and hearing. Our eyes and ears are the sensory organs best adapted to artistic perception. Both observe and then spur the mind to consider and respond.

Although an artist does most of the communicative work in a film, a spectator must contribute as well by actively sorting through his perceptions. Critics and spectators once thought that film viewing could be nothing but a passive experience, and indeed at its worst it is. But a good film calls forth vigorous sensory and intellectual activity. The time of a film is a period of intensely concentrated experiences demanding the full

attention and imagination of a viewer. On one level a viewer partici-
pates physically in a film. That is, his senses authenticate illusions and
tell the mind it must deal with a sensible, integrated whole even though
enormous geographical and chronological leaps are present. Consequently
a viewer can physically feel sensations of anger or fear while accepting
spans of time and distance. On a higher level a viewer responds through
emotions and, most important of all, through imagination. By perceiving
the plight of another or by realizing his own foibles, a viewer's sympa-
thetic imagination is charged.

IMAGINATIVE PARTICIPATION

The human imagination is sparked. That is why reason and imagination
are always separated. Our reason may say "if I give that beggar a dime, I'll
be ten cents poorer"; our imagination will move us beyond strictly logical
consequences and assert our humanness, perhaps saying "I could be in
that guy's shoes, and I should give him a dime because he looks so desti-
tute." Imagination is the wellspring of emotion, and the movie theater
provides an excellent setting to have emotions evoked. The spectator sits
in darkness, relying for orientation on the images appearing on the screen.
That is why the process of film viewing is often compared to a dream.
Mysterious things can happen in a darkened theater where a thousand
people can each be alone.

When film energizes the imagination a person does, at times, seem
spellbound. The magic of film can captivate and hold a viewer's attention. But magic must move outward to clarify complexities of the world
and to challenge the imagination—unless entertainment is the sole intent.
Active visual and oral confrontation tends to jell both ideas and emotions.

At the same time, film has limitations in its ability to lead viewers
to an idea. Preconceptions largely govern how people will see, hence
determining responses to cinematic images. Many commentators thought,
for example, that most Americans would be morally outraged at Mayor
Daley's police for the way they conducted themselves during the Chicago
Democratic convention of 1968. Yet most Americans vigorously supported
the police and staunchly backed cops beating demonstrators. There is a
lesson in the response of the public. A film must be carefully put together
to escape viewer predilections or prejudices even when it tries to be absolutely honest. The truth of what happened at that convention is highly
complicated (as the hundreds of pages of the riot commission's report
suggest). But the response of the public was simple and direct—and based
more on prior allegiances than on information. To deal with the nuances
of the Chicago convention would require an extraordinarily skillful filmmaker. Film rhetoric is as necessary to disseminate truth as it is to create

falsehoods. Raw images simply do not necessarily convey reality to an audience.

Not perceiving what we see is an old problem of viewing. Prior experience and orientation contribute heavily to our process of understanding. Most people, for instance, have experienced the confusion brought about when their senses tell them one thing and their intellect another. When walking in a house tilted at a twenty-degree angle, for example, one's intellect tells him that the house is tilted but his senses suggest even more strongly that he is walking at an angle. The geometry of a house provides a frame of reference saying "level and square" to the senses, while the intellect knows a house can be tilted. It is the conflict between sensory and intellectual response that creates the disorientations of carnival fun houses.

In the movie theater a viewer must continually distinguish between physical and psychological realities and illusions. While responding to characters on the screen, a viewer will experience strong feelings of joy, love, affection, hate, outrage, and so on. But a viewer never tries to embrace the hero or heroine or hit the villain. The same emotions experienced in life would lead to action, yet the intellect tells the imagination that its perceptions do not convey reality. In the movie house, viewers can feel emotions with consequences more capable of control than in life. Viewers can, for instance, enjoy horrors and chills by seeing monsters or goblins they would not enjoy confronting in actuality.

Filmmakers treat emotions at different levels according to purpose and audience. Some films rhetorically create emotion for its own sake, arousing then satiating a viewer. Most mass-entertainment films are of this type, asking the viewer to shed tears or feel joy and then releasing him to go about his daily business as if joy or tears have no more consequence for his life than a good massage.

Some films, however, exploit emotion to lead a viewer to a particular opinion. The State Department, for example, makes films (to be distributed only in foreign countries) emotionally persuading foreign viewers of the rightness of the Vietnam war. Newsreel, a group of leftist film cooperatives, similarly manipulates emotions to try to persuade people of the injustice of the Vietnam war and of the corruptness of the American system. Both the State Department and Newsreel exploit emotions to propagandize particular goals.

A third sort of film also exists, one usually called the "art film." Although it can be of any genre from western to love story, this sort of film attempts neither to pander to an audience and exploit emotions for financial gain nor to exploit for propaganda reasons. Rather, the art film explores emotions and in so doing often helps men to come to grips with their own lives or to make some meaningful sense out of the absurdity and chaos of the. world. This sort of film makes the largest demands on the viewer. The imagination must be highly activated to understand most art films because such films ask a viewer to confront seriously some part of himself or of the world.

The art film is coming to dominate film production more and more. Television now has lifted from cinema the burden of entertaining and proselytizing to a mass audience. Consequently film continues to move more and more toward art and a serious coming to grips with the rhythms of experience. Because it has such great potential emotional and intellectual force, film has a high challenge to provide a blinded world with vision. And an audience has an equally strong challenge to grasp the rhetoric of film and consequently to possess the tools necessary to understand and respond critically to the most important artistic medium of the twentieth century. As George Linden suggests, "Motion pictures, like dreams or rainbows, are true myths that we tell ourselves so that we may try to come to grips with what life means in the living of it."[2]

[2] *Reflections on the Screen* (Belmont, California: Wadsworth Publishing Co., 1970), p. 229.

GLOSSARY
OF FILM TERMS

Animation The process of photographing drawings or objects a frame at a time; by changing a drawing or moving an object slightly before each frame is taken, the illusion of motion is realized.

Auteur (French for "author"); literally the director, who is regarded as the "author" of a film because he has primary control and responsibility for the final product. The **Auteur** theory insists that a film be considered in terms of the entire canon of a director and that each **Auteur** earns that title by displaying a unique cinematic style.

Back Projection (See **Rear Projection.**)

Background Music Music accompanying action on the screen, but coming from no discernible source within the film.

Blocking The arrangements made for the composition of a scene, especially the placement and movements of actors.

Boom A long mobile beam or pole used to hold a microphone or camera.

Cinéma Vérité A candid-camera style of filmmaking using handheld cameras, natural sound, grainy high-contrast black-and-white film, and the appearance of no rehearsal and only basic editing.

Cinematographer (cameraman or director of photography) The person who supervises all aspects of photography from the operation of cameras to lighting.

Clip A brief segment excerpted from a film.

Commentator A voice (the person speaking may be either seen or unseen) commenting on the action of a film. A commentator, unlike a narrator, provides supposedly unbiased information, maintaining apparent perspective and distance from what occurs on the screen.

Composition The placement of people or objects within the frame and the arrangements for actual movements within the frame or by the camera.

Continuity The narrative growth of a film created through a combination of visuals and sound (resembling the "story" in print literature).

Continuity Sketches (See **Storyboard.**)

Crane Shot A shot taken from a **boom** that can move both horizontally and vertically.

Cross-Cutting (parallel editing) A method of editing in which action switches alternately from events at one location or time to those of another.

Cut An individual strip of film consisting of a single shot; the separation of two pieces of action as a "transition" (used when one says "cut from the shot of the boy to the shot of the girl"); a verb meaning to join shots together in the editing process; or an order to end a take ("cut!").

159

Cutter   (See **Editor.**)

Dailies   (See **Rushes.**)

Deep Focus (depth photography) Keeping images close by and far away in sharp focus simultaneously.

Depth of Field The area within which objects are in focus; a large depth of field allows a great range of objects to be in focus simultaneously, while a shallow depth of field offers a very limited area in focus. Depth of field normally depends on how far "open" a lens is (a lens works much like an eye, with the pupil opening or contracting to control light). An "open" lens (for example, f 1.4) creates a shallow depth of field while a "stopped down" (contracted) lens (for example f 16) creates a large depth of field.

Director The person responsible for overseeing all aspects of the making of a film.

Dissolve (lap dissolve) A method of making a transition from one shot to another by briefly superimposing one image upon another and then allowing the first image to disappear. A dissolve is a stronger form of transition than a **cut** and indicates a distinct separation in action.

Dolly A platform on wheels serving as a camera mount capable of movement in any direction.

Dolly Shot A moving shot taken from a **dolly.** A **Dolly-In** moves the camera toward the subject, while a **Dolly-Out** moves the camera away from the subject. A dolly shot creates a sense of movement through space by capturing changes in perspective.

Double Exposure (superimposition) Two distinct images appearing simultaneously with one superimposed upon the other.

Dubbing (lip sync) The process of matching voice with the lip movements of an actor on the screen; dubbing also refers to any aspect of adding or combining sounds to create a film's final soundtrack.

Editing (continuity editing, narrative montage) The process of splicing individual shots together into a complete film. Editing (as opposed to **Montage**) puts shots together to create a smoothly flowing narrative in an order making obvious sense in terms of time and place.

Editor (cutter) The person responsible for assembling the various visual and audial components of a film into a coherent and effective whole.

Fade A transitional device in which either an image gradually dims until the viewer sees only a black screen (**Fade-Out**) or an image slowly emerges from a black screen to a clear and bright picture (**Fade-In**). A fade provides a strong break in continuity, usually setting off sequences.

Fast Motion (accelerated motion) Movements on the screen appearing more rapid than they would in actual life. For example, a man riding a bicycle will display legs pumping furiously while he flashes through city streets at the speed of a racing car. A filmmaker achieves fast motion by running film through his camera at a speed slower than the standard 24 frames per second; subsequent projection of 24 frames per second speeds up the action.

Fill Light Light used to control shadows by "filling in" certain dark areas.

Film Stock Unexposed strips of celluloid holding light-sensitive emulsions.

Filters   Transparent glass of gelatin placed in front of or behind a lens to control coloration; some filters cut out certain types of light (such as ultra-violet); others create a soft, hazy appearance, and still others provide a dominant color when used with color films.

Fine Cut   The final assembling of all the various audial and visual components of a film.

Fish-Eye   An extreme wide-angle lens taking in (and distorting) an immense area.

Flashback   A segment of film that breaks normal chronological order by shifting directly to time past. Flashback may be subjective (showing the thoughts and memory of a character) or objective (returning to earlier events to show their relationship to the present).

Flash Forward   A segment of film that breaks normal chronological order by shifting directly to a future time. Flash forward, like **flashback,** may be subjective (showing precognition or fears of what might happen) or objective (suggesting what will eventually happen and thus setting up relationships for an audience to perceive).

Flashframe   A shot lasting only a few frames; the shortness of a flashframe makes its content difficult to assimilate. When many flashframes follow each other, they create a feeling of intense action and often visually resemble the effects of stroboscopic light; when used alone, flashframes usually act as **flashbacks** or **flash forwards.**

Flip   A transitional device (now used rarely) in which an image appears to flip over, revealing another image on its backside; the effect is much like flipping a coin from one side to the other.

Focal Length   The distance from the focal point of a lens to the plane of the film (for viewers and cameramen, this is seen as the amount of area a lens can photograph from a given distance.)

Focus-Through   (racking)   A change of the field in focus taking the viewer from one object to another that was previously out of focus.

Frame   A single photographic image imprinted on a length of film; also the perimeter of an image as seen when projected on a screen (a filmmaker sees the frame as the boundaries of his camera's view-finder).

Freeze Frame   A single frame repeated for an extended time, consequently looking like a still photograph.

High-Angle Shot   A shot taken from above a subject, creating a sense of "looking down" upon whatever is photographed.

Iris   A technique used to show an image in only one small round area of the screen. An **Iris-Out** begins as a pinpoint and then moves outward to reveal the full scene, while an **Iris-In** moves inward from all sides to leave only a small image on the screen. An iris can be either a transitional device (using the image held as a point of transition) or a way of focusing attention on a specific part of a scene without reducing the scene in size.

Jump Cut   An instantaneous cut from one action to another, at first seemingly unrelated, action. A jump cut can also be any poorly made cut causing a noticeable jump in action.

Key Light   The primary source of illumination **High-Key** light brilliantly illuminates a set; **Low-Key** light provides dim lighting, usually with heavy, dark shadows.

Lap Dissolve   (See **Dissolve**.)

Library Shot (stock shot)   Any shot not taken for a particular film but used in it.

Lip Sync   (See **Dubbing**.)

Local Music   Music originating within a scene and audible to both the characters in the film and the audience.

Location   A place outside the studio where shooting occurs.

Long Lens   Any lens with a **focal length** greater than normal; a normal focal length approximates the size relationships seen by the human eye, while a long focal length creates a narrower angle of vision, causing a larger image. A long lens alters perspective by flattening a subject into its background. (See **Telephoto**.)

Loop Film   A film with ends joined, creating a loop that can be run continuously through a projector.

Low-Angle Shot   A shot taken from below a subject, creating a sense of "looking up to" whatever is photographed.

Mask   A device placed in front of a lens to reduce the horizontal or vertical size of the frame or to create a particular shape (for example, periscope eyepiece, binoculars, or gunsight).

Match Cut   A cut intended to blend two shots together unobtrusively (opposed to a **Jump Cut**).

Matte Shot   A process for combining two separate shots on one print, resulting in a picture that looks as if it had been photographed all at once. For example, a shot of a man walking might be combined with a shot of a card table in such a way that the man appears to be six inches high and walking on a normal size card table.

Metteur-En-Scène   A director or filmmaker (often used to indicate a director who does not deserve the title **auteur**).

Mise-En-Scène   The aura emanating from details of setting, scenery, and staging.

Mix   The process of combining all sounds at their proper levels from several tracks and placing them onto a master track.

Montage (dynamic editing, expressive montage, conditional montage)   A method of putting shots together in such a way that dissimilar materials are juxtaposed to make a statement. A shot of a man followed by a shot of a peacock, for example, declares that the man is pompous. (See **Editing**.)

MOS   Any segment of film taken without sound. (The letters **MOS** come from early foreign directors who wanted pictures taken "mit out sound.")

Moviola   A special projection machine (used by film editors) that holds several reels of film simultaneously and can run at variable speeds, backward or forward, and stop at any frame. (Moviola was originally a brand name but now refers only to a type of projection machine.)

Negative Image   An image with color value reversed from positive to negative, making white seem black and black appear white.

Neorealism A film style using documentary techniques for fictional purposes. Most neorealist films rely on high-contrast black-and-white film, nonprofessional actors, and natural settings. Neorealism began as a movement among a group of filmmakers in Italy after World War II.

New Wave (*Nouvelle vague*) A recent movement in French filmmaking based mainly on the notion of the **auteur**. The movement was begun in the late 1950s by a group of young filmmakers (including François Truffaut, Jean-Luc Godard, Louis Malle, and Alain Resnais) interested in exploring new potentials for film art.

Nonsynchronous Sound Sound that combines sounds from one source with visuals from another, such as intense argument with only a man walking alone visible, or the sounds of a rooster accompanying visuals of a classroom lecturer. (See **Synchronous Sound**.)

Objective Camera The attempt to suggest that the camera acts only as a passive recorder of what happens in front of it. The use of objective camera relies on deemphasis of technique, involving minimal camera movement and editing.

Optical Printer A device used to "print" the images of one film onto another film through direct photography.

Out-Take A take that is not included in the final version of a film.

Pan A shot in which a stationary camera turns horizontally, revealing new areas.

Parallel Editing (See **Cross-Cutting**.)

Perspective The way objects appear to the eye in terms of their relative positions and distances.

Pixillation A technique using cartoon methods to create movement by objects or people. For example, a man will stand with feet together and be photographed, then he will repeat this action over and over, but move slightly forward each time; the result will show the man apparently moving forward (usually rapidly) without moving any part of his body.

Process Shot A shot coordinated with another image created by **Rear Projection**, making the resulting picture look like a single simultaneous shot. A typical process shot shows the faces of two people riding in a car; behind them (as seen through the rear window) moves the usual traffic of a city street. The traffic has been added by rear projection, creating a process shot.

Producer The person who is responsible for all of the business aspects of making and releasing a film.

Racking (See **Focus-Through**.)

Reaction Shot A shot showing one or more characters reacting to an action or statement.

Rear Projection (back projection) The process of projecting an image onto a translucent screen from the back side rather than over the heads of the viewers as is usually done. Filmmakers use rear projection to film an action against a projected background, thus recording on film both the stage action and the rear-projected image. (See **Process Shot**.)

Reverse Angle Shot A shot of an object or person taken in the direction opposite that of the preceding shot (for example, a shot of the gates of a prison from within followed by a reverse angle shot showing the gates from outside).

Rough Cut   The initial assembling of the shots of a film, done without added sound.

Rushes (dailies)   The lengths of footage taken during the course of filming and processed as the shooting of a film proceeds.

Scenario   (See **Script.**)

Scene   A series of **Shots** taken at one basic time and place. A scene is one of the basic structural units of film, with each scene contributing to the next largest unit of film, the **sequence.**

Script (scenario, shooting script)   A written description of the action, dialogue, and camera placements for a film.

Sequence   A structural unit of a film using time, location, or some pattern to link together a number of **scenes.**

Shooting Ratio   The ratio in a finished film of the amount of film shot to the length of the final footage.

Shot   A single uninterrupted action of a camera as seen by a viewer (see **Take**). Shots are labeled according to the apparent distance of the subject from the camera: extreme long-shot (ELS) also called an establishing shot; long-shot (LS); medium long-shot (MLS); medium or mid-shot (MS); medium close-up (MCU); close-up (CU); and extreme close-up (ECU). Although distinctions among shots must be defined in terms of the subject, the human body furnishes the usual standard of definition: ELS, a person is visible but setting dominates; LS, person fills vertical line of the frame; MLS, knees to head; MS, waist up; MCU, shoulders up; CU, head only; ECU, an eye.

Slow Motion   Movements on the screen appearing slower than they would in actual life. For example, a diver will seem to float to the water gently rather than fall at the speed dictated by gravity. A filmmaker achieves slow motion by running film through his camera at a speed faster than the standard 24 frames per second; subsequent projection at 24 frames per second slows down the action.

Soft Focus   A slightly blurred effect achieved by using a special filter or lens, or by shooting with a normal lens slightly out of focus.

Still   A photograph taken with a still (versus motion) camera.

Stock Shot   (See **Library Shot.**)

Storyboard (continuity sketches)   A series of sketches (resembling a cartoon strip) showing potential ways various shots might be filmed.

Subjective Camera   Shots simulating what a character actually sees; audience, character, and camera all "see" the same thing. Much subjective camera involves distortion, indicating abnormal mental states. Shots suggesting how a viewer should respond are also called "subjective" (for example, a high-angle shot used to make a boy look small and helpless).

Superimposition   (See **Double Exposure.**)

Swish Pan   A quick **pan** from one position to another caused by spinning the camera on its vertical axis and resulting in a blurring of details between the two points. Sometimes a swish pan is used as a transition by creating a blur and then ending the blur at an action in an entirely different place or time.

Synchronous Sound   Sound coordinated with and derived from a film's visuals. (See **Nonsynchronous Sound.**)

Take   A single uninterrupted action of a camera as seen by a filmmaker. A take is unedited footage as taken from the camera, while a shot is the uninterrupted action left after editing.

Telephoto Lens   (See **Long Lens.**) A lens with an extremely long focal length capable of making distant objects appear nearer and thus larger. (A telephoto has greater power of magnification than a **Long Lens.**)

Tilt Shot   A shot taken by angling a stationary camera up (**tilt-up**) or down (**tilt-down**).

Tracking Shot   (traveling shot, trucking shot)   Any shot using a mobile camera that follows (or moves toward or away from) the subject by moving on tracks or by being mounted on a vehicle.

Trailer   A short segment of film that theaters use to advertise a feature film.

Trucking Shot   Any moving shot with the camera on a mobile mounting, but chiefly a moving shot taken with a camera mounted on a truck.

Two Shot   A shot of two people, usually from the waist up.

Voice-Over   Any spoken language not seeming to come from images on the screen.

Wide-Angle Lens   Any lens with a focal length shorter than normal, thus allowing a greater area to be photographed. A wide-angle lens alters perspective by making nearby objects seem relatively larger than those far away and by increasing the apparent distance between objects both laterally and in depth.

Wipe   A transitional device in which one image slowly replaces another by pushing the other out of the way.

Zoom Freeze   A **zoom shot** that ends in a **freeze frame.**

Zoom Shot   A shot accomplished with a lens capable of smoothly and continuously changing focal lengths from **wide-angle** to **telephoto** (**zoom in**) or telephoto to wide-angle (**zoom out**).

FURTHER READING

INTRODUCTORY WORKS

Bobker, Lee R. *Elements of Film.* New York: Harcourt Brace & Jovanovich, 1969.

Casty, Alan Howard. *The Dramatic Art of Film.* New York: Harper & Row, 1970.

Gessner, Robert. *The Moving Image: A Guide to Cinematic Literacy.* New York: Dutton, 1968.

Huss, Roy, and Silverstein, Norman. *The Film Experience.* New York: Harper & Row, 1968.

Lawson, John Howard. *Film: The Creative Process.* New York: Hill and Wang, 1964.

Lindgren, Ernest. *The Art of the Film.* 3d ed. New York: Macmillan, 1968.

Renan, Sheldon. *An Introduction to the American Underground Film.* New York: Dutton, 1967.

Stephenson, Ralph, and Debrix, J. R. *The Cinema as Art.* Baltimore: Penguin, 1965.

Whitaker, Rod. *The Language of Film.* Englewood Cliffs, N.J.: Prentice-Hall, 1970.

FILM THEORY AND ESTHETICS

Arnheim, Rudolph. *Film as Art.* Berkeley: University of California Press, 1957.

Balazs, Bela. *Theory of the Film.* New York: Roy Publishers, 1953.

Bazin, André. *What Is Cinema?* Berkeley: University of California Press, 1967.

Eisenstein, Sergei. *Film Form.* New York: Harcourt Brace & Jovanovich, 1949.

_____. *The Film Sense.* New York: Harcourt Brace & Jovanovich, 1942.

Kracauer, Siegfried. *Theory of Film.* New York: Oxford, 1960.

Linden, George W. *Reflections on the Screen.* Belmont, Calif.: Wadsworth, 1970.

MacCann, Richard Dyer, ed. *Film: A Montage of Theories.* New York: Dutton, 1966.

Pudovkin, Vsevolod. *Film Technique and Film Acting.* Trans. and ed. by Ivor Montagu. New York: Grove Press, 1960.

Reisz, Karel. *The Technique of Film Editing.* New York: Hastings House, 1968.

Youngblood, Gene. *Expanded Cinema.* New York: Dutton, 1970.

FILM HISTORY

Anderson, Joseph, and Richie, Donald. *The Japanese Film: Art and Industry.* New York: Grove Press, 1960.

Brownlow, Kevin. *The Parade's Gone By.* New York: Knopf, 1969.

Fulton, A. R. *Motion Pictures: The Development of an Art.* Norman, Okla.: University of Oklahoma Press, 1960.

Jacobs, Lewis. *The Rise of the American Film.* New York: Harcourt Brace & Jovanovich, 1939.

Knight, Arthur. *The Liveliest Art.* New York: Macmillan, 1957.

Kracauer, Siegfried. *From Caligari to Hitler.* Princeton: Princeton University Press, 1947.

MacGowan, Kenneth. *Behind the Screen.* New York: Dell, 1965.

Mast, Gerald. *A Short History of the Movies.* New York: Bobbs-Merrill, 1971.

COLLECTIONS OF FILM REVIEWS

Agee, James. *Agee on Film: Reviews and Comments.* Boston: Beacon Press, 1964.

Kael, Pauline. *I Lost It at the Movies.* Boston: Little, Brown, 1965.

_____. *Kiss Kiss Bang Bang.* Boston: Little, Brown, 1968.

Kauffmann, Stanley. *A World on Film.* New York: Dell, 1966.

Macdonald, Dwight. *Dwight Macdonald on Movies.* Englewood Cliffs, N.J.: Prentice-Hall, 1969.

Sarris, Andrew. *Confessions of a Cultist: On the Cinema, 1955/1969.* New York: Simon and Schuster, 1970.

Simon, John. *Private Screenings.* New York: Macmillan, 1967.

EXAMINATIONS OF FILMS AND FILMMAKERS

Armes, Roy. *The Cinema of Alain Resnais.* New York: A. S. Barnes, 1968.

Barry, Iris. *D. W. Griffith: American Film Master.* New York: Museum of Modern Art, 1965.

Bogdanovich, Peter. *The Cinema of Alfred Hitchcock.* New York: Museum of Modern Art, 1963.

_____. *The Cinema of Howard Hawks.* New York: Museum of Modern Art, 1962.

_____. *The Cinema of Orson Welles.* New York: Museum of Modern Art, 1961.

_____. *John Ford.* Berkeley: University of California Press, 1970.

Cameron, Ian, ed. *The Films of Jean-Luc Godard.* New York: Praeger, 1970.

_____. *The Films of Robert Bresson.* New York: Praeger, 1970.

_____, and Wood, Robin. *Antonioni.* New York: Praeger, 1969.

Cowie, Peter. *The Cinema of Orson Welles.* New York: A. S. Barnes, 1965.

Donner, Jorn. *The Personal Vision of Ingmar Bergman.* Bloomington, Ind.: Indiana University Press, 1964.

Durgnat, Raymond. *Luis Buñuel*. Berkeley: University of California Press, 1970.

Gibson, Arthur. *The Silence of God: Creative Response to the Films of Ingmar Bergman*. New York: Harper & Row, 1969.

Gottesman, Ronald, ed. *Focus on "Citizen Kane."* Englewood Cliffs, N.J.: Prentice-Hall, 1971.

Higham, Charles. *The Films of Orson Welles*. Berkeley: University of California Press, 1970.

Huss, Roy, ed. *Focus on "Blow-Up."* Englewood Cliffs, N.J.: Prentice-Hall, 1971.

Kyrou, Ado. *Luis Buñuel*. Trans. Adrienne Foulke. New York: Simon and Schuster, 1963.

McCaffrey, Donald W. *Focus on Chaplin*. Englewood Cliffs, N.J.: Prentice-Hall, 1971.

Mussman, Toby, ed. *Jean-Luc Godard*. New York: Dutton, 1968.

Richie, Donald. *The Films of Akira Kurosawa*. Berkeley: University of California Press, 1970.

Roud, Richard. *Godard*. New York: Doubleday, 1968.

Salachas, Gilbert. *Frederico Fellini*. New York: Crown, 1969.

Silva, Fred, ed. *Focus on "The Birth of a Nation."* Englewood Cliffs, N.J.: Prentice-Hall, 1971.

Steene, Birgitta. *Ingmar Bergman*. New York: Twayne, 1968.

Taylor, John Russell. *Cinema Eye, Cinema Ear: Some Key Film-makers in the Sixties*. New York: Hill and Wang, 1964.

Truffaut, François, with Helen G. Scott. *Hitchcock*. New York: Simon and Schuster, 1966.

Ward, John. *Alain Resnais, or The Theme of Time*. New York: Doubleday, 1968.

INTERVIEWS WITH FILMMAKERS

Geduld, Harry M., ed. *Filmmakers on Film Making: Statements on Their Art by Thirty Directors*. Bloomington, Ind.: Indiana University Press, 1967.

Gelmis, Joseph, ed. *The Film Director as Superstar*. Garden City: Doubleday, 1970.

Levin, G. Roy. *Documentary Explorations: Fifteen Interviews with Film-makers*. Garden City: Doubleday, 1971.

Sarris, Andrew, ed. *Interviews with Film Directors*. New York: Bobbs-Merrill, 1967.

FILM AND LITERATURE

Bluestone, George. *Novels into Film*. Berkeley: University of California Press, 1957.

Marcus, Fred H., ed. *Film and Literature: Contrasts in Media*. Scranton, Pa.: Chandler, 1971.

Nicoll, Alardyce. *Film and Theater*. New York: Crowell, 1936.

Richardson, Robert. *Literature and Film*. Bloomington, Ind.: Indiana University Press, 1969.

FILM AND EDUCATION

Katz, John Stuart. *Perspectives on the Study of Film*. Boston: Little, Brown, 1971.

Poteet, G. Howard. *The Compleat Guide to Film Study*. Urbana, Ill.: National Council of Teachers of English, 1971.

Sheridan, Marion C., et al. *The Motion Picture and the Teaching of English*. New York: Appleton-Century-Crofts, 1965.

Stewart, David C. *Film Study in Higher Education*. Washington, D.C.: American Council on Education, 1966.

FILMMAKING

Livingston, Don. *Film and the Director*. New York: Macmillan, 1953.

Pincus, Edward. *Guide to Filmmaking*. New York: New American Library, 1969.

Robert, Kenneth H., and Sharples, Win, Jr. *A Primer for Film-making*. New York: Bobbs-Merrill, 1971.

REFERENCE

Cowie, Peter. *International Film Guide*. New York: A. S. Barnes, 1972. A valuable yearly compilation of information on production, festivals, films released on 8mm and 16mm, magazines, film services, and so on.

Gottesman, Ronald, and Geduld, Harry M. *Guidebook to Film: An Eleven-in-One Reference*. New York: Holt, Rinehart and Winston, 1972. An indispensable guide to information necessary for film study; besides offering the most comprehensive and best organized bibliography of books about film, *Guidebook to Film* provides information about museums and archives, film schools, equipment and supplies, distributors, bookstores, sources for stills, film organizations, festivals, and awards.

Halliwell, Leslie. *The Filmgoer's Companion*, 3d ed. rev. New York: Hill and Wang, 1970. A useful one-volume encyclopedia of film information.

MAJOR 16mm
FILM DISTRIBUTORS

Anyone ordering films will find *Feature Films on 8mm and 16mm,* 3d edition (New York: R. R. Bowker), by James L. Limbacker, an indispensable aid for locating distributors of particular films. In addition, *Mass Media* (a bi-weekly newsletter available from Mass Media Associates, 2116 N. Charles Street, Baltimore, Maryland 21218) provides up-to-date listings of important films put into 16mm distribution.

American Documentary Films
379 Bay Street
San Francisco, Calif. 94133
415/982–7475
336 West 84th Street
New York, N.Y. 10024
212/799–7440

Audio/Brandon
34 MacQuesten Parkway So.
Mount Vernon, N.Y. 10550
914/664–5051
406 Clement Street
San Francisco, Calif. 94118
415/752–4800
1619 North Cherokee
Los Angeles, Calif. 90028
213/463–0357
8615 Director's Row
Dallas, Texas 75247
214/637–2483
512 Burlington Avenue
LaGrange, Ill. 60525
312/482–9090

AVCO Embassy Pictures Corp.
1301 Avenue of the Americas
New York, N.Y. 10019
212/956–5500

Canyon Cinema Cooperative
Room 220
Industrial Center Building
Sausalito, Calif. 94965
415/332–1514

Center Cinema Co-op
540 North Lakeshore Drive
Chicago, Ill. 60611
312/664–6824

Cinema 5 Ltd.
595 Madison Avenue
New York, N.Y. 10022
212/421–5555

Cine World
13 Arcadia Road
Old Greenwich, Conn. 06870
203/637–4319

Columbia Cinematheque
711 Fifth Avenue
New York, N.Y. 10022
212/751–7529

Contemporary/McGraw-Hill Films
Princeton Road
Hightstown, N.J. 08520
609/448–1700
828 Custer Avenue
Evanston, Ill. 60202
312/869–5010
1714 Stockton Street
San Francisco, Calif. 94133
415/362–3115

Creative Film Society
8435 Geyser Avenue
Northridge, Calif. 91324
213/786–8277

Film-Makers' Cooperative
175 Lexington Avenue
New York, N.Y. 10016
212/889-3820

Films Incorporated
35-01 Queens Boulevard
Long Island City, N.Y. 11101
212/937-1110

Box 11707
Atlanta, Ga. 30305
404/237-0341

161 Massachusetts Avenue
Boston, Mass. 02115
212/937-1110

1414 Dragon Street
Dallas, Texas 75207
214/741-4071

Suite 1
98 West Jackson Street
Hayward, Calif. 94544
415/782-4777

5625 Hollywood Boulevard
Hollywood, Calif. 90028
213/466-5481

4420 Oakton Street
Skokie, Ill. 60076
312/676-1088

Grove Press Film Division
53 East 11th Street
New York, N.Y. 10003
212/677-0002

Janus Films
745 Fifth Avenue
New York, N.Y. 10022
212/753-7100

Mass Media Associates
2116 North Charles Street
Baltimore, Maryland 21218
301/727-3270

1720 Chouteau Avenue
St. Louis, Missouri 63103
314/436-0418

Museum of Modern Art Film Library
11 West 53d Street
New York, N.Y. 10019
212/956-6100

New Line Cinema
121 University Place
New York, N.Y. 10003
212/674-7460

Newsreel
Room 101
1232 Market Street
San Francisco, Calif. 94102
415/621-6196

New Yorker Films
2409 Broadway
New York, N.Y. 10024
212/362-6330

Pyramid Films
Box 1048
Santa Monica, Calif. 90406
213/828-7577

Swank Motion Pictures
201 South Jefferson Avenue
St. Louis, Mo. 63166
314/534-6300

Twyman Films
329 Salem Avenue
Dayton, Ohio 45401
513/222-4014

United Artists 16
729 Seventh Avenue
New York, N.Y. 10019
212/245-6000

United Films
1425 South Main
Tulsa, Okla. 94119
918/584-6491

Universal/16
445 Park Avenue
New York, N.Y. 10022
212/759-7500

Walter Reade 16
241 East 34th Street
New York, N.Y. 10016
212/683-6300

Warner Bros., Inc.
Non-Theatrical Division
4000 Warner Boulevard
Burbank, Calif. 91505
213/843-6000

INDEX